THE FLOATING ISLAND PLAYS

THE FLOATING ISLAND PLAYS

EDUARDO MACHADO

THEATRE COMMUNICATIONS GROUP
1991

The Floating Island Plays is published by Theatre Communications Group, Inc.,
355 Lexington Ave., New York, NY 10017.

TCG gratefully acknowledges public funds from the National Endowment for
the Arts, the New York State Council on the Arts and the New York City
Department of Cultural Affairs in addition to the generous support of the fol-
lowing foundations and corporations: Alcoa Foundation; Ameritech
Foundation; ARCO Foundation; AT&T Foundation; Citibank, N.A.;
Consolidated Edison Company of New York; Nathan Cummings Foundation;
Dayton Hudson Foundation; Exxon Corporation; Ford Foundation; James
Irvine Foundation; Jerome Foundation; Andrew W. Mellon Foundation;
Metropolitan Life Foundation; National Broadcasting Company; Pew
Charitable Trusts; Philip Morris Companies; Scherman Foundation; Shubert
Foundation.

Cover art "Mares" copyright © 1985 by Inverna Lockpez

Machado, Eduardo.
    The floating island plays / Eduardo Machado.—1st ed.
    Contents: The modern ladies of Guanabacoa—Fabiola—In the eye of the
hurricane—Broken eggs.
    ISBN 1-55936-035-6 (cloth) — ISBN 1-55936-034-8 (paper)
    1. Cuban Americans—Drama.   I. Title
PS3563.A31154F58   1991
812' .54—dc20   91-23117
                                                     CIP

First Edition: November 1991

*For Phoebe
and her master*

CONTENTS

THE FLOATING ISLAND PLAYS

THE MODERN LADIES OF GUANABACOA

For Harriett

And to the memory of my grandfather,
Oscar Hernandez,
a victim of history

CHARACTERS

MARIA JOSEFA, a Cuban woman, short, attractive, in her late forties
ARTURO, her husband, a Basque
MANUELA, their daughter, in her mid-twenties
ERNESTO, their eldest son
MARIO, their second son
MIGUEL, their youngest son
DOLORES, Maria Josefa's friend
ADELITA, Ernesto's wife, a very light mulatta
OSCAR HERNANDEZ, a taxi driver, thirty years old

TIME

Act One: a spring day in 1928.
Act Two: a summer day in 1931.

PLACE

A middle-class home in Guanabacoa, Cuba.

THE MODERN LADIES OF GUANABACOA

ACT ONE

Guanabacoa, Cuba, 1928. A middle-class home, Spanish in style, built at the end of the last century. The living room and dining room of the house are seen downstage center, with a door from the dining room leading to the offstage kitchen. The front door of the house, stage right, opens off the living room onto a small front porch, and there is a large back porch stage left. Both porches give access to the street. Manuela's bedroom is seen upstage center. A hallway leads to an offstage bathroom and to the other bedrooms of the house.

Manuela is sitting in the living room, looking at a fashion magazine. Maria Josefa enters. She is smoking a cigarette.

MANUELA: Short hair! Short hair! Short hair! Mama, the answer to all my prayers.

MARIA JOSEFA: The neighbors still talk about my cigarettes. What would they say about short hair?

MANUELA: That it's wicked, that only women of ill repute do it.

MARIA JOSEFA: No short hair. No.

MANUELA: Nuns cut their hair!

MARIA JOSEFA: Nuns do it as a sacrifice to the Lord Jesus and the Virgin Mary. To show they're not vain about earthly things, not for style's sake. That's different.

MANUELA: Look, Mama, cool this summer. It'll be so convenient. Easy to take care of when I'm working.

MARIA JOSEFA (*Glancing at magazine*): Beautiful, stylish; look how it looks when they curl it; your father would never allow it.

MANUELA: I'm twenty-seven. I should have a say.

MARIA JOSEFA: As long as you live under his roof and above his floor, you have to do what he likes. Always remember that. Memorize what I just told you. He feels bad enough about Ramon.

MANUELA: What about Ramon!! I'm the one that should feel bad.

3

MARIA JOSEFA: Father only worries. Ramon and you were engaged for seven years, then you didn't get married, and he worries about that all the time.

MANUELA: It's not my fault, Mama. He died. (*She sobs*)

MARIA JOSEFA: Yes, but what man wants another man's bride.

MANUELA: I'm a good girl. I'll be a virgin on my wedding night.

MARIA JOSEFA: Did he kiss you? Manuela, did Ramon kiss you?

MANUELA: Mama!! Don't embarrass me.

MARIA JOSEFA: Tell me, did Ramon kiss you before he died, Manuela?

MANUELA: Yes, Mama, he did.

MARIA JOSEFA: Your father's right. I'm a terrible chaperone. Men are haunted by things like that. Men want their women to only have kissed them; you should know that. Do not tell your father.

MANUELA: Oh, someone has a hex on me. It's not my fault. (*She prays silently and beats her breast three times*) Oscar has been saying hello to me.

MARIA JOSEFA: Oscar Hernandez?

MANUELA: Yes, the taxicab driver, Estrella's cousin?

MARIA JOSEFA: He works for Americans.

MANUELA: No.

MARIA JOSEFA: That's what people say, they're always saying that he drives Americans around all day long. That's what they say about him.

MANUELA: He drives a taxicab!

MARIA JOSEFA: Manuela, your father wants you to marry a man with a business. Just because your brother married trash...

MANUELA: I think she's nice.

MARIA JOSEFA: Ah, mulatta. (*She makes the sign of the cross*) Pray to God my grandson turns out light.

MANUELA: She's light. You can hardly tell.

MARIA JOSEFA: I can tell. Your father won't consent till he approves of your choice; but when he approves it'll be the right man.

MANUELA: Where's Papa, anyway? He's late for lunch.

MARIA JOSEFA: Eating with a business acquaintance—business.

MANUELA: Who?

MARIA JOSEFA: Let me see the magazine. (*Takes magazine*) Oh, what I like are the dresses and the pearls hanging so far down. Oh, especially the black mark by the lip. Exotic, but refined. The man who sells him eggs.

MANUELA: Please, Mama, let's cut it. We'll be the modern ladies of Guanabacoa.

THE MODERN LADIES OF GUANABACOA

MARIA JOSEFA: They already say I'm trying to be a Yankee because of the cigarettes.

The clock strikes twelve.

MANUELA: What's wrong with that; they're the richest nation in the world.

MARIA JOSEFA: They're a bunch of gangsters. Manuela, lunch! Your brother will be here in a flash.

MANUELA: Who's eating?

MARIA JOSEFA: Just Mario; Miguel is eating out.

MANUELA: Or having affairs, no doubt.

MARIA JOSEFA: He's a young man; they have special needs. Young ladies shouldn't and don't understand the needs young men have.

They exit into kitchen. We hear talking offstage. Mario and Miguel enter. They're whispering.

MARIO: How do you know it was him; maybe it was someone that looked like him.

MIGUEL: Who else in Cuba is that tall? Blond, blue eyes and speaks with a Basque accent.

MARIO: He shouldn't do things like that in town; what if someone else saw him?

MIGUEL: She seduced him; he couldn't say no; what do you expect, he's a man.

MARIO: But the gringo's wife; he should be careful. He overbought again too many eggs, five extra pigs. He's such a fool.

MIGUEL: You should feel proud; because Father is the greatest stud in the province of Havana.

MARIO: He fools around, we take care of the business, he overbuys to prove that he's running a successful store, then he goes out into the street and conquers while we work.

Manuela and Maria Josefa enter with food.

MIGUEL: What are we having today?

MARIA JOSEFA: Fried bananas, rice and baked fish. Don't worry, Miguel, there's plenty for you.

MANUELA: Did the young lady not serve hot lunch today?

MARIO: Manuela! That dress shows too much.

MANUELA: Too much of what?

MARIO: Your breast. People will talk. You have to be careful.

MANUELA: Oh. I'm sorry.

MARIA JOSEFA: Pay attention to your brothers. It's their reputation at stake.

MIGUEL: No one wants a trollop for a sister.

MARIO: Do not use that language! Have respect for your mother and sister, Miguel!

MARIA JOSEFA: Manuela wanted to cut her hair.

MARIO: You said no.

MIGUEL: Only Yankees cut their hair.

MANUELA: Let me serve you lunch, Mario.

MARIO: Thank you, sister.

MANUELA: How much fish?

MARIO: Just a little bit.

MARIA JOSEFA: Aren't you hungry?

MIGUEL: I am.

MARIO: That's enough.

MARIA JOSEFA: I'll serve you.

MIGUEL: Thank you, Mama.

MARIO: That's plenty. Where's Father?

MARIA JOSEFA: With a business acquaintance. Didn't he tell you?

MARIO: Oh, yes. The man who sells...

MANUELA: Eggs.

MIGUEL: Yes, eggs.

MARIA JOSEFA: No more talk.

They eat, except Manuela, who continues to serve, pouring water, etc.

MARIO: Mama, the fish doesn't have enough salt.

MIGUEL: I think it needs pepper.

MARIO: I can't eat it.

MARIA JOSEFA: I'll fry you two eggs; they go well with rice—and bananas.

MARIO: You don't have to, but if you want to, fine.

MARIA JOSEFA: Of course, my darling. I'm glad your father isn't here to taste it. And you, Miguel, do you like it? Can you eat it?

MIGUEL: I'm fine.

Maria Josefa exits to the kitchen.

Has anyone heard from Ernesto?

MANUELA: He's married now. (*She giggles*)

THE MODERN LADIES OF GUANABACOA

MARIO: That shouldn't matter; a child's first duty is to his parents. It's one of the commandments. No man can love any woman as much as his own mother, because no woman on earth suffered the way she did to give him life. Even Christ loved his mother more than mankind.

MIGUEL: Manuela, another piece of fish.

She takes his plate, serves him.

MANUELA: Is that enough?

MIGUEL: A little more. Thank you.

MANUELA: My pleasure.

MARIO: Manuela, always remember, a daughter's loyalty is first to her father. That's whose name you carry to your death.

MANUELA: In America, they get their husband's name.

MARIO: Americans! Manuela! No matter who you marry, first is your father, then your family, then your husband.

MANUELA: No one will ever take Papa's place.

Maria Josefa enters.

MARIA JOSEFA: Two eggs, my darling. I sprinkled lots of salt. Here's some fresh rice. Do you want me to mix them for you?

MARIO: Yes, Mama, you're a saint.

She mixes them and feeds Mario.

MARIA JOSEFA: My two handsome boys; now taste it. Is it good, Mario, yes?

MARIO: Hmmmmmm. (*He nods yes*)

MARIA JOSEFA: Manuela, Mario's dirty plates. Into the kitchen.

Manuela takes Mario's dirty plates.

MIGUEL: And bring back some more water.

MARIA JOSEFA: And start boiling water for café.

MANUELA: All right. (*She exits*)

MARIA JOSEFA: Do you really like it?

MARIO: Delicious.

MARIA JOSEFA: I have some sad and shocking news that I feel I must tell you. I talked to Dolores Gutirez. And now you two must do something about it.

Mario and Miguel look at each other in terror.

MIGUEL: What?

MARIO: She's just a gossip.

MARIA JOSEFA: She saw Adelita dancing with another man.

MARIO: Where?

MIGUEL: Adelita?

MARIA JOSEFA: The mulatta.

Manuela enters.

MIGUEL: Ernesto's wife!

MARIO: God damn it, shit damn.

MANUELA: What's wrong?

They eat.

What about Ernesto's wife?

They eat.

What happened?

MARIA JOSEFA: Let's eat.

MARIO: Thank you, Mama. We'll take care of her.

MANUELA: What did she do?

MIGUEL: She was seen tangoing with—

MARIA JOSEFA: Quiet.

MIGUEL: Never mind, sorry, Mama.

MARIO: Just don't spend a lot of time with her; be polite, you're her sister-in-law. She's pregnant with our brother's baby.

MARIA JOSEFA: Maybe!

MARIO: But don't trust her.

MANUELA: What has she done?

MARIA JOSEFA: She's making a cuckold out of your brother; she's putting horns on his head. (*She begins to cry*)

MANUELA: Oh God, poor Ernesto.

MIGUEL: She's been doing it in public, tangoing with a strange man.

MARIA JOSEFA: Enough talk, eat.

Silence.

The tango. Oh, help us, sweet blessed heart of Jesus Christ.

MARIO: Yes, Mama, you're right.

MIGUEL: Mama's always right, right?

MARIO: I'll set her straight. No brother of mine is going to be cuckolded.

MANUELA: We should tell him, he should know.

MARIO: Leave it to us.

MIGUEL: We know what to do.

MARIA JOSEFA: No more discussions.

Manuela finally starts to eat.

Manuela, help me bring in the café.

Manuela and Maria Josefa exit.

MARIO: Slut, she'd better confess.

MIGUEL: We'll get his name, and we'll beat the shit out of him. In the balls where it hurts.

MARIO: If she only danced with him we won't tell Ernesto. We'll just warn her and tell her it better not happen again. If there was more, we'll tell Ernesto and he can decide what to do.

MIGUEL: She's sneaky. How will we know she's telling the truth?

MARIO: We'll get his name from her, and the truth from him.

Maria Josefa carries a tray with four cups of café. Manuela follows.

MARIA JOSEFA: Café, boys, café.

They each take a cup and drink it in one gulp.

MARIO: Delicious.

MIGUEL: Now a nap.

MARIO: At work in a half-hour.

MANUELA: Don't worry, Mario. I'll wake him.

Miguel exits.

MARIO: I have information to trace, Mama. Thank Dolores for us. Tell her to please keep it between us and her and make something nice for dinner.

Mario exits, Manuela eats, Maria Josefa sips her café.

MARIA JOSEFA: Let's clear the dishes and the girl will do them later.

MANUELA: I'm so worried.

MARIA JOSEFA: Don't think about it; your brothers will take care of it.

They gather the dishes.

MANUELA: I think the fish tastes fine.

MARIA JOSEFA: Mario likes special attention, that's all. He's a little spoiled; I spoiled him; he'll find a good wife.

MANUELA: What would we do without him and Papa.

They clear the dishes onto a tray.

Mama, I have a confession...

MARIA JOSEFA: What is it, Manuela?

MANUELA: Well, you see...

MARIA JOSEFA: Tell me, Manuela!

MANUELA: Oscar is coming today, to ask permission. To call on me in the evenings.

MARIA JOSEFA: When did he ask you? Where did you speak to him, when?

MANUELA: At the dance for "Our Lady of the Immaculate Conception."

MARIA JOSEFA: Do you know him? Did Mario speak to him?

MANUELA: Yes, he did. He asked me to dance five times.

MARIA JOSEFA: Did he kiss you?!

MANUELA: No, Mama, he did not!

MARIA JOSEFA: He was polite?

MANUELA: Yes. He wants to call on me, he said he'd come by and ask permission. He's a gentleman, Mama, he's handsome.

MARIA JOSEFA: Hope your father likes him, let's hope he likes him.

MANUELA: Let's pray that he likes him. I like him.

MARIA JOSEFA: Be proper, remember, be proper.

MANUELA: I will. You raised me right. Can I try a cigarette?

MARIA JOSEFA: All right, but don't tell your father. He knows I smoke but never in front of him.

They smoke cigarettes.

You're right, Manuela, short hair is attractive. I bet it looks great with cigarettes.

MANUELA: It does, Mama, look at this picture. (*She pulls her hair up and poses with a cigarette*)

MARIA JOSEFA: We'll mention it to your father. He likes his two ladies to be up-to-date.

MANUELA: It's truly European.

MARIA JOSEFA: That won't help with Arturo the Basque.

Manuela winds the Victrola. It plays. They smoke and look at the magazine. Arturo enters.

ARTURO: Put out the cigarettes, I want lunch in ten minutes, I'm hungry.

MARIA JOSEFA: I thought they took you out to lunch.

ARTURO: He only bought me drinks.

MANUELA: I'll make you a banana omelet.

MARIA JOSEFA: And warm up the rice.

ARTURO: Thank you, my sweet girl.

Arturo blows Manuela a kiss. She catches it, then exits to the kitchen with tray of dishes.

Now I need a clean shirt.

MARIA JOSEFA: It's not hot today. I have things to talk to you about. Oscar Hernandez wants to call on Manuela. What do you think?

ARTURO: Did you give him permission?

MARIA JOSEFA: He's coming today to ask you for permission.

ARTURO: Fine, dear.

MARIA JOSEFA: We were thinking of cutting our hair in a bob like they're doing now; it's the latest style, and I want to be in style so you never get bored. So you never want anything else, so you never go looking anywhere else, so you don't have a roving eye. Adelita was seen tangoing with a man. Mario's looking into it. What is Ernesto going to do? I wonder if it's his baby?

ARTURO: Just gossip, don't listen to gossips.

MARIA JOSEFA: But you have to check things out. I don't want my son to be a cuckold. I want our family to be respected. I never danced with anyone but you, not for thirty-four years. I was fourteen. You're the handsomest man, they all look like cockroaches next to you. I love you. I adore you, only you. (*She is standing next to him*) You smell like perfume.

ARTURO: Manuela! Is lunch ready.

MANUELA: Not yet, Papa.

MARIA JOSEFA: You do, you smell like perfume.

ARTURO: It's the combination of my cologne and sweat. That's why I need a fresh shirt.

MARIA JOSEFA: I'll help Manuela. Hurry up.

Arturo exits to the bathroom and Maria Josefa to the kitchen. There is a knock at the door. Manuela enters, opens the door.

MANUELA: Oscar. Let me call my mother.

OSCAR: Yes, of course. I'll wait outside.

MANUELA: Mama. Mama, come here for a moment.

Maria Josefa enters.

MARIA JOSEFA: What is it? (*She goes to the door*) Oh, Oscar, please come in.

OSCAR: People talk in this town, but they don't talk about you and they never will. You are so proper.

MARIA JOSEFA: Thank you.

MANUELA: Thank you.

OSCAR: Columbus said Cuban women are the most beautiful and chaste. You are the image he was talking about.

MANUELA: Thank you, Oscar.

MARIA JOSEFA: Yes. Would you like to sit down? Café? A cold glass of water? Anything.

OSCAR: Thank you. But I have to get back to work. I came to ask for permission, if I may come tonight and call on Manuela. If I may?

MARIA JOSEFA: Well, it's up to her father.

OSCAR: To the butcher shop, thank you.

MANUELA: No, he's here! I'll get him.

OSCAR: Don't wake him!

MANUELA: He's not taking a nap. (*She exits*)

MARIA JOSEFA: Can I get you some dessert, lemonade, crackers?

OSCAR: No thank you, I'm fine.

MARIA JOSEFA: Do you mind if I smoke?

OSCAR: Not at all, I think it's attractive.

MARIA JOSEFA: It's one of my few vanities.

MANUELA: He'll be here in a minute.

ARTURO (*Offstage*): Wake up, my lazy son, wake up.

MIGUEL (*Offstage*): Shit! Oh sorry, Papa.

ARTURO (*Offstage*): Get to work. (*He enters*) Yes.

OSCAR: Well, sir, I would like to call on your daughter tonight.

ARTURO: Fine. Be here at eight-thirty; be out of here at ten.

OSCAR: Thank you, sir.

Miguel enters, Maria Josefa exits to the kitchen.

MIGUEL: You didn't wake me, Manuela, I'm late.

MANUELA: You said half an hour.

MIGUEL: I have to get to work. (*He exits*)

OSCAR: Till eight-thirty, sir. Till eight-thirty, Manuela.

MANUELA: Yes, Oscar.

OSCAR (*Exiting*): I'll drive you, Miguel.

ARTURO: Lunch, Manuela.

MANUELA: Yes, Papa. Thank you.

MARIA JOSEFA: Here is your lunch.

Arturo eats.

MANUELA: Anything else?

ARTURO: Just for you to sit by me. You'll be my girl forever, won't you.

MANUELA: Yes, Papa, forever.

ARTURO: I hear you want to cut your hair.

MANUELA: Yes.

MARIA JOSEFA: I don't know. . .

MANUELA: It's in style, styles change.

Maria Josefa looks through the magazine.

MARIA JOSEFA: Maybe she's right, but is it feminine?

MANUELA: I think so, please, Papa.

ARTURO: Maybe, we'll talk about it later.

MANUELA: Please, Papa!

ARTURO: But I like my sweet girl's long hair.

DOLORES (*On the porch*): It's me, Maria, have a glass of water for an old friend?

ARTURO: Dolores the gossip, your source of information.

MARIA JOSEFA: Be quiet. Don't embarrass me, please. Arturo, you know about her husband and the nightclub singer in Havana. Please be polite. Please. (*She goes to answer the door*)

DOLORES: Maria.

They kiss.

My sweet poor dear friend.

Arturo exits to the kitchen.

MARIA JOSEFA: Good news, Manuela has an appointment tonight. Oscar Hernandez the taxicab driver, Estrella's cousin. What do you think?

DOLORES: Does he know about Ramon?

MARIA JOSEFA: He must. He was at the funeral.

DOLORES: That's right. Ramon and he went to school together; he's very handsome, a little... you know. (*She indicates by touching her skin that he is dark*)

MARIA JOSEFA: No, he's light, you can hardly tell. It was his great-great-grandmother's mother.

Arturo enters with a glass of water on a plate, and gives it to Dolores.

ARTURO: The Moors conquered you Spaniards for five hundred years.

DOLORES: Arturo, having lunch. It's so late.

ARTURO: A businessman's life is hurried nowadays.

DOLORES: Yes, the business.

ARTURO: Running a business is hard work.

Arturo eats one bite of his omelet. Dolores looks at him.

Well. I'm done. I'm going.

MANUELA: No café? You hardly ate. Was the omelet overdone?

ARTURO: Later, sweetheart.

DOLORES: Walk your father to work, keep him company.

ARTURO: Why?

DOLORES: You'll miss her when she's married and not yours anymore.

MANUELA: It'd be nice to take a walk.

ARTURO: Come then. I like having pretty girls walking me down the street.

DOLORES: You do, don't you?

ARTURO: Goodbye, Dolores, see you again. Goodbye, sweetness, I'm working late.

MARIA JOSEFA: Be sure to come in time to see Oscar, please. He'll be here at eight-thirty.

ARTURO: I'll be home at ten.

MARIA JOSEFA: Goodbye, dear.

Arturo and Manuela exit.

I'll get us café.

DOLORES: Sit down, Maria, take a deep breath. I have some sad news.

MARIA JOSEFA: What? It's not Ernesto's baby.

DOLORES: I just have to say it fast because it breaks my heart. I saw Arturo with Beatrice the American. They went into a hotel. They used the room for two hours. I'm sorry I had to tell you, but I am your friend.

MARIA JOSEFA: It was him and her?

DOLORES: Yes.

MARIA JOSEFA: Thank you, Dolores. My family is dishonored. (*She finishes Dolores's water*) Café?

DOLORES: No. Do you need anything?

MARIA JOSEFA: No, thank you. (*She gets a cigarette and lets her hair down. She looks at herself in the mirror*) There's no portrait of me, no record of my youth except what people remember. I dreamed Arturo caressed me, I caressed him back. It was as simple as that. My compulsions. My sorrow gets in the way.

DOLORES: Should I stay with you for a moment?

MARIA JOSEFA: Yes. It's my fault, I've tried to be good.

DOLORES: You are good.

MARIA JOSEFA: Can I tell you a secret? Between us? Between just these walls?

DOLORES: Of course, we've been friends all our lives.

MARIA JOSEFA: I was so afraid not to follow the rules that I never found the essence.

DOLORES: The essence—there's no essence. That's the table, it's there; the sun is warm, you feel it, you have a home, you get fed. It's real. It's life.

MARIA JOSEFA: And afterwards, there's heaven?

DOLORES: Of course.

MARIA JOSEFA: And we'll levitate.

DOLORES: We'll float up to Christ.

MARIA JOSEFA: And he'll caress our faces and stroke our hair, feel our pulse and cover us with kisses.

DOLORES: He blows into your mouth to bring you back to life, but that's when he comes back, and we get our bodies back. After death just your spirit floats up.

MARIA JOSEFA: And we float because we followed his rules.

DOLORES: Yes.

MARIA JOSEFA: It's worth the wait.

DOLORES: Yes, dear.

MARIA JOSEFA: Yes it is.

They kiss. Maria Josefa goes to the mirror and looks at her hair. She touches it.

THE FLOATING ISLAND PLAYS

A caress, that's what life is. It's pretty. It's still pretty.

Blackout. Lights up. Maria Josefa, Manuela, Mario, Miguel and Ernesto are sitting at the table eating custard. Maria Josefa is sitting next to Ernesto.

MIGUEL: This guy walks up to another guy. He says, "How much do you weigh?" The other guy answers, "A hundred and sixty-five pounds exactly." The other guy shoots him. Bang. Bang. The guy who shot tells the other guy, "A hundred and sixty-five pounds and two ounces."

No one laughs.

The bullet weighed two ounces. BANG! BANG!

Some of them laugh.

ERNESTO: Where's Papa?
MARIO: Working.
ERNESTO: Oh, I see, poor Papa.
MARIA JOSEFA: Manuela, eat something.
MANUELA: I'm nervous!
MIGUEL: Because of her beau.
ERNESTO: Oscar! Oscar! Oscar!
MARIO: Where's your wife?
MARIA JOSEFA: Not now.
ERNESTO: At her mother's. I have a free night. (*He laughs*)
MARIO: At her mother's. Oh, you left her there?
ERNESTO: Of course. Two farmers go to a big theatre in Havana. They get seats far away from each other. One farmer says to the other farmer, "As soon as the show is over, find me so we don't miss the bus." They sit. The show is over. The one farmer gets up and yells, "José, we're going to miss the bus." A lady goes up to him and says, "Sir, this is a respectable theatre, please don't yell." The farmer says, "I have to find José." The lady says, "Here, use my binoculars." He finds José. He looks like he's standing right there. He whispers, "José, we're going to miss the bus."

They laugh.

MARIO: You're picking her up.
ERNESTO: Of course, more custard.

THE MODERN LADIES OF GUANABACOA

MIGUEL: Oh, Oscar, my love.

MANUELA: Stop it.

MARIA JOSEFA: Stop it, Miguel!

Miguel starts to sing.

Too bad for your father, he's missing all the fun but it must be worth it.

MARIO: What?

MARIA JOSEFA: His business.

MARIO: Of course, it keeps us alive.

ERNESTO, MARIO AND MIGUEL (*Singing*):
Days dancing free and in love.
Hours full of passion and song.
The days and the hours
that we wait.
For that one look
full of passion and song.

Days filled with endless desire.
Hours when desire turns to pain.
The pain of the hours that we wait.
For that one look
full of passion and song.

MANUELA: Stop it Ernesto, Miguel.

ERNESTO: My favorite, most beautiful lady, your married son still has to come home for a good dinner.

MARIA JOSEFA: Do you think I'm beautiful?

ERNESTO: Like an Italian painting.

MIGUEL: It's hard to find a woman that compares with you.

ERNESTO: When I went to school, no mother was ever like you.

MARIA JOSEFA: Oh, I've gotten old. But I do have handsome sons who'll take care of me, yes?

ERNESTO: Yes, Mama.

MIGUEL: Till we hit our graves.

MARIA JOSEFA: Hold my hand, Miguel. Hold my hand, Ernesto. And keep me company, before anyone else, before wives and children and girlfriends.

ERNESTO: Always, Mama. Always. (*He kisses her on the forehead*)

MIGUEL: Yours, Mama.

MARIA JOSEFA: Let's clear the table.

The women clear as the men light cigars and smoke.

MARIO: Two guys are at a bullring. Across the way one of the guys sees a beautiful girl. He tells his friend, "Look, I'm going to marry that girl." His friend asks, "Which one?" The guy points at her again. "That one over on the other side." The friend asks, "Which one?" The guy takes out his gun. Bang. Bang.

Oscar knocks on the front door, Mario goes to answer it.

Oscar.

OSCAR: Mario.

MARIO: Pleasure to see you.

ERNESTO: Oscar.

OSCAR: Ernesto.

MIGUEL: Oscar, thanks for the ride.

MARIO: I'll get Mama.

MIGUEL: Ernesto, I'll be out on the porch.

ERNESTO: Dominos?

MIGUEL: Of course. (*He exits to porch*)

OSCAR: How's married life?

ERNESTO: Oh all right, you know women.

OSCAR: Yes.

Maria Josefa enters.

ERNESTO: See you later on.

OSCAR: Good evening, Maria, how are you tonight.

Ernesto exits to porch and plays dominos with Miguel.

MARIA JOSEFA: Fine. Fine. Manuela.

MANUELA (*Offstage*): Yes.

MARIA JOSEFA: Oscar is here.

Manuela enters.

OSCAR: Good evening. Wonderful to see you.

MANUELA: The same.

Mario walks through on his way to the porch.

THE MODERN LADIES OF GUANABACOA

MARIA JOSEFA: Mario, sit with them while I get the café.
OSCAR: Ah, café. Thank you.
MARIO: Come and sit.

Oscar waits for Manuela to sit first, then Mario sits, then Oscar. They all stare at each other smiling for about two minutes. Once in a while Manuela and Oscar look at each other for a second.

OSCAR: What a comfortable sofa.
MANUELA: Yes.
OSCAR: Ah, the smell of café.

Maria Josefa enters with cups of café on a tray.

MARIA JOSEFA: Excuse me, Oscar, I'll serve the boys first, then we can sit and talk.
OSCAR: No trouble.
MARIO: Are you sure?
OSCAR: I'm positive.

Maria Josefa goes to the porch.

MARIO: What would we do without café.
OSCAR: Yes, café. It used to be a religious drink.
MANUELA: Really.

Maria Josefa enters.

MARIA JOSEFA: Oscar?
OSCAR: Thank you. (*He smells his café*) The aroma.
MARIA JOSEFA: Mario. (*Gives him café*)
MARIO: Thank you.
OSCAR: It was discovered under—
MARIO: I'm going outside for a while.
OSCAR: —very interesting circumstances.
MARIA JOSEFA: And one for Manuela.
MANUELA: And one for you.

Maria Josefa sits.

OSCAR: It's still like a religious service.
MARIA JOSEFA: What is.
MANUELA: Café, Oscar was talking about café.

MARIA JOSEFA: Oh. Café. Yes?

OSCAR: The name derives from the Arabic "Kahwah."

MANUELA: Kahwah?

OSCAR: Kahwah makes an aromatic beverage which is very valued which is made into brew with toasted and ground coffee seeds. In the thirteenth century a preaching Arabian mulatto observed how the cows after they ate the fruits of some trees became animated. He noticed a certain activity which departed from the norm and that it was a direct result from the trees and leaves they were eating. Well, the Arab, after noticing, prepared, with the grain of the before-mentioned kahwah, a brew which became a part of his religious ceremonies. The results were stupendous. His followers were able to stay awake through all the religious services.

MANUELA: How interesting, Oscar.

OSCAR: Since then, the use of coffee became generalized in Egypt's Pergia. It was introduced in Europe in 1660, passing through the French Antilles and later to South America.

MARIA JOSEFA: You must read a great deal. Mario, come in here. It's very interesting. Miguel, Ernesto, you too.

They come in and stand by the door.

MANUELA: I'm sorry, Oscar, we must be embarrassing you.

OSCAR: Not at all, dear. Anyway. . .

MANUELA (*To herself*): Dear. (*She smiles*)

OSCAR: As the years passed, coffee began to become a habit according to the different customs of each different country. In each country, it had a special characteristic. In some countries, a small cup of coffee is used to welcome visitors.

MANUELA: Like here in Cuba.

OSCAR: It's become more frequent an expression these days. To offer a small cup of aromatic café is to bring a note of courtesy to a reunion.

MARIA JOSEFA: Beautifully said, almost poetic, Oscar. (*She signals the boys to sit*)

OSCAR: In Europe as well as America, coffee shops became famous, where scholars and students seated around a table with their respective cups of aromatic café discussed very passionately, politics, literature, poetics and art. Some of these establishments, like. . .Merchants' Coffee House, have become a part of history.

MANUELA: Really?

OSCAR: It was there in 1717, no 1774, a "Committee of Correspondence," started by New Yorkian patriots, sent a letter to a group of Bostonians proposing the union of American colonies.

MARIO: Very interesting.

ERNESTO: And they drink such weak coffee.

MARIO: Like dirty water.

MIGUEL: I could never drink it.

MANUELA: Shh.

MARIA JOSEFA: Continue.

OSCAR: Well, today the producers of the fabulous bean are Colombia, Brazil—

MANUELA: Not just us?

OSCAR: —Guatemala, El Salvador, Mexico, Costa Rica, Honduras, Haiti, Santo Domingo, Puerto Rico, Cuba.

MARIO: For the best!!

OSCAR: True, but it's even cultivated in Ethiopia.

MANUELA: Ethiopia, Africa!!

OSCAR: Yes, today in the entire world, one always savors a small cup of the brown nectar from the white gods.

They applaud.

MARIA JOSEFA: So well put, I'm making another round. Bring in the cups.

MARIO: I'll get mine.

ERNESTO (*Simultaneously*): Make mine with milk, Mama.

The three go into the kitchen; Miguel stays and chaperones. Manuela looks at him.

MIGUEL: Me too. (*He exits to the kitchen*)

Oscar gives Manuela a note.

OSCAR: I adore you.

They kiss.

MANUELA: My love.

MARIA JOSEFA (*Offstage*): In the kitchen, children.

MANUELA: On our way, Mama.

They go into the kitchen. Arturo enters; he goes to bedrooms. We hear running water. Maria Josefa enters. In the kitchen, Miguel is telling jokes we heard earlier.

MARIA JOSEFA: Taking a shower so late at night?

The water stops. Arturo comes into the living room.

Your sons are here. Where were you?

ARTURO: Working, darling, my sweetheart, working.

MARIA JOSEFA: They're in the kitchen. Say hello to Oscar.

Arturo goes into the kitchen. Maria Josefa sits on the front porch in a place where the rest won't see her when they enter. She lights a cigarette, leaves the front door open.

ARTURO (*Offstage*): Miguel, Mario, Ernesto, say hello to your father. Oscar, good evening. Manuela, let the men talk for a while.

Manuela enters and goes into her bedroom.

MANUELA: Oscar, Oscar, Oscar Hernandez. The lips feel nice. (*She gets lipstick, rubs it on*) Oh what a thought. I won't have to wait anymore. Oh what a thought. Oscar Hernandez.

The men enter the living room.

ERNESTO: The store was quiet, we did not sell enough again today. We are not making enough money.

ARTURO: It'll get better.

ERNESTO: I don't know, Papa, you are buying too much; today we received twenty dozen eggs from Paco, when you know we only sell ten.

ARTURO: I owe Paco a favor, he is my friend, what's an extra couple of dozens.

MARIO: If you keep overbuying we will not make it this month. I still haven't taken my salary for last week. You owe me a week!

ARTURO: You two have to learn, men help each other that's how the world got this far. Have pride. What's a couple of dozen eggs? Pride, that's life.

MARIO: We are ordering too much.

ARTURO: We'll discuss this at work not at home, goodnight. (*To Oscar*) Ten o'clock. (*He exits*)

OSCAR: Goodnight, sir. Ernesto, the problem is not overbuying, it's knowing what to sell.

MARIO: What to sell, that's right; Ernesto, Oscar's right.

ERNESTO: We sell meat.

MANUELA: Enough business for one night.

OSCAR: It's important, Manuela, it is the future; I'll see you tomorrow at eight-thirty.

MANUELA: At eight.

OSCAR: Then at eight, whatever you say.

MANUELA: Goodnight.

OSCAR: Sleep well.

She exits.

MARIO: Don't say goodnight to your brothers.

She comes back and kisses her brothers on the forehead. She exits.

OSCAR: The business for the decade of the thirties is transportation. Transportation.

ERNESTO: Transportation?

MARIO: Taxis?

OSCAR: No, bigger than that; buses, you can carry thirty passengers, five cents a ride.

ERNESTO: Highways, yes.

OSCAR: To Havana and back. Five of us have talked to the transportation authority, and they're going to give us the routes in the province of Havana. All I need is capital and they'll give me my own routes. That's my plan.

MARIO: Let's go to a bar. Oscar? Ernesto?

ERNESTO: Yes, let's do that.

OSCAR: I have my taxi, ready to go?

ERNESTO: Five cents a ride?

MARIO: Miguel!

MIGUEL: Yes?

MARIO: To a bar.

MIGUEL: All right.

OSCAR: The automobile, no more trains or boats or horses. Transportation, that's the money in the future.

They exit. Maria Josefa enters the living room.

MARIA JOSEFA: The future, the thirties. Youth, hope, ambition. Hope, no remorse, without lies. Who defeats my fiercest foes? Who revives my fainting heart? Who is life in life to me? What's the high reward I win? Whose name do I glory in?

Arturo enters in his robe.

ARTURO: To bed, dear.

MARIA JOSEFA: Not now, not ever. I won't ever touch you. I won't ever touch a man. I won't ever look at you. I'm tired of being confused. I'm tired of being tormented.

ARTURO: What are you talking about?

MARIA JOSEFA: A hotel room at lunch before dinner; sneaking off with Americans. Adultery; being made a fool!

ARTURO: You shouldn't listen to gossips.

MARIA JOSEFA: Because gossips tell the truth. Because gossips see and report it. Because gossips see you deceiving me. I never had another man touch me. I've always stayed at home. I get up early and make the café, boil the milk, wash the clothes, keep everyone clean, prepare the lemonade. I do the job.

ARTURO: And I've always been discreet. I'll always keep it out of your eyes, out of the house, that's what men are supposed to do. Let's go to sleep.

MARIA JOSEFA: No I have something to do. I'm getting rid of this. (*She touches her hair*)

ARTURO: I give my permission. Goodnight. (*He exits*)

MARIA JOSEFA: I did the job twelve times. Arturo de la Asuncion Ripoll born July 16, 1895. Died at birth. Ernesto born June 7, 1898. Manuela born January 1, 1901, she grew up to be his true love. Mario born December 22, 1906. Fernando de la Asuncion Ripoll born July 23, 1907, died October 30, 1907. Gilda de la Asuncion Ripoll born May 29, 1909, died June 10, 1909, Miguel born March 10, 1911, Pepe de la Asuncion Ripoll born March 7, 1912, died four months later, Antonia de la Asuncion Ripoll born April 22, 1913, died December 23, 1913, all the babies that went from the womb to the breast to the grave. I had no milk, so they died. Olga de la Asuncion Ripoll born November 18, 1915, born dead, and the one that was early and died the next day, Eurgenio de la Asuncion Ripoll. Enrique born November 14, 1902. Died aged eleven, December 26, 1913. There was something wrong with his blood. That is my life with him and he talks about discretion. (*She gets scissors*) Manuela dear, wake up. Father gave us his permission. We're cutting our hair. We are going to be in style, dear.

Blackout.

END OF ACT ONE

THE MODERN LADIES OF GUANABACOA

ACT TWO

Three years later. 1931. The set is the same but all the furnishings, which are Art Deco in style, are new. Arturo, Maria Josefa, Manuela, Adelita and Dolores are in the living room. The women all have short hair and are dressed like flappers. Manuela is nine months pregnant. The song "Sheik of Araby," sung by Rudi Vallee, is playing on the Victrola.

ARTURO: What is he saying?

ADELITA: It's a tribute to Valentino. They idolized him in the USA; they like exotic pepole.

MARIA JOSEFA: Tell me, Adelita, is it the custom in America . . . to leave the only grandson at the mother's mother's house?

ADELITA: He fell asleep, I didn't want to wake him.

DOLORES: Discover Cuba first, and North America later.

ADELITA: Delicious meal, Maria.

MANUELA: I cooked it, Adelita.

DOLORES: Good for you, Manuela, this family is full of hard-working people.

ARTURO: Did Oscar tell you when he was coming back, Manuela?

MANUELA: No, Papa.

ARTURO: Adelita, did Ernesto tell you when they were coming back?

MARIA JOSEFA: They should be here soon, Ernesto told me it was an important meeting.

DOLORES: Arturo, you must miss the butcher shop.

ARTURO: No, Dolores, I count the money at night. It's my job to guard the equipment. I protect the buses at night.

DOLORES: They shot two people in Havana last night.

MARIA JOSEFA: You know politicians, they don't even believe in Baby Jesus.

DOLORES: Oh Manuelita, you're so big, Manuelita pregnant.

ARTURO: Don't talk about it in front of me, I feel like hitting Oscar in the face.

Sound of buses pulling up. Horns honk.

MANUELA: Papa!

DOLORES: She's married now.

MARIA JOSEFA: She's expecting exactly nine months after the wedding night.

ADELITA: Just like me.

THE FLOATING ISLAND PLAYS

We hear the men humming "We're in the Money": La La La Money/ La La La Money/ La La La La La La, La La La Money. The men enter.

ERNESTO: He did it! The transportation cooperative approved the request.

OSCAR: We have our dream.

ADELITA: I want to go for a ride.

MARIO: Not bad, Papa, we did it, two more buses.

MIGUEL: You want to see them?

ARTURO: No, everybody inside the house.

ERNESTO: He'll want another meeting.

ADELITA: Please, I want to go for a ride.

ERNESTO: Later, Adelita, not now. Papa wants us inside the house.

DOLORES: Two more buses, this family is on its way, will you remember your neighbors?

OSCAR: Always, Dolores. What kind of people do you think we are?

ARTURO: I need to talk to the men, time for business, you ladies go somewhere and talk.

DOLORES: I'll go to my house and leave the family alone, so you can celebrate.

MARIA JOSEFA: No, stay.

DOLORES: I'll talk to you tomorrow, goodnight. Congratulations, Oscar.

OSCAR: Thank you.

Dolores exits.

MANUELA: I have to take a nap. I get tired all the time, nine months.

OSCAR: Are you happy?

MANUELA: Yes, Oscar. I'm glad about the buses. I'll ride one of them after the baby's born. (*She exits to the bedroom*)

MARIA JOSEFA: I'll be in the kitchen, there's dessert. Call me when you want it.

ERNESTO: What kind?

MARIA JOSEFA: Rum cake. (*She clears the table*)

ADELITA: Let me help you, Maria. (*She starts to help her*)

MARIA JOSEFA: That's all right, Adelita, I can do it. I'll take care of the dishes. (*She exits*)

ADELITA: Yes, of course. I'm sorry.

Adelita goes. It is quiet for a moment.

THE MODERN LADIES OF GUANABACOA

ARTURO: So what do we get?

OSCAR: All the routes from Guanabacoa to Havana and the ones to Cojimar and they promised later on another bus and the routes to Regla.

ARTURO: I know the government is going to want a cut.

OSCAR: The government has been taken care of.

ARTURO: You talked to them?

OSCAR: Not directly.

ARTURO: You, Ernesto?

ERNESTO: No.

ARTURO: I like the way you take care of my money!

MARIO: Your money is in good hands; we are doing what we promise.

ARTURO: Who talked to them?

OSCAR: The cooperative, and they assured me that the government will
not interfere. Arturo, all those pale, white Americans are saving any
money they earn, to throw it all away for two weeks in the sun and
the beach.

ARTURO: In the USA the market crashed.

OSCAR: Father, brothers, this is the most beautiful land that human eyes
have seen. It was true when Christopher Columbus said it and it's
true today. And Americans will spend anything they have for fun and
the sun and we have that here in Cuba.

MIGUEL: We have the only safe business, Papa.

Maria Josefa enters.

MARIA JOSEFA: Are you done? Is all the business taken care of? Who wants
cake? You, Arturo?

ARTURO: No, I'll be leaving soon. It's my night to guard the equipment.
They're not putting me out to pasture, I still have to work.

MIGUEL: You're still the bull, Papa.

ERNESTO: Mama, I want a great big piece of cake.

MARIA JOSEFA: My darling. I'll bring you a great big piece.

ERNESTO: I'll go with you. I'll taste it in the kitchen, then eat it in the living room.

Ernesto and Maria Josefa exit to the kitchen.

ARTURO: Your Yankee ideals will never work.

OSCAR: Free enterprise is knowing how to follow the plan. I know how.

ARTURO: Capitalism is falling apart. That's what a depression is.

OSCAR: We're not. You find what people want, need; be ready to get it; you charge them; they'll always pay it. Then you succeed anywhere at any time.

ARTURO: My father was a sheepherder. He never changed. My town stayed the same through the last war, Napoleon, the Moors. We live high up in the mountains and though Spain claims us as theirs, their territory, we know we're not. We know we're a tribe unto ourselves. We believe in no one. We know who we are.

OSCAR: Were you poor?

ARTURO: We ate.

OSCAR: Eating isn't enough anymore. We need different things. They've invented the automobile, a washing machine, a light bulb; and it's not what you eat anymore, it's how you cook it. Not just food, what kind of plates you eat it on—

We hear Adelita singing.

—what forks you are using, on what kind of table—pine or mahogany. And we have to buy it. That's all.

ARTURO: I never had a thought like that. Never.

OSCAR: That's all right, I have.

ARTURO: Oscar? Rum? Brandy?

OSCAR: No, thank you.

Arturo, Miguel and Mario drink their brandy; Oscar goes out to the front porch; Adelita is sitting there singing.

Adelita.

ADELITA (*Sings*): May I look for the one who is pure, may I keep all the things that endure. . .

OSCAR: I saw you.

ADELITA: So.

OSCAR: So? That's all you have to say, so.

ADELITA: No. So what!

OSCAR: What!

ADELITA: It means so what that you saw me. I saw you, too. What were you doing there?

OSCAR: Having a few drinks.

ADELITA: So was I.

OSCAR: What if somebody else saw you?

ADELITA: Then they saw me, so what.

OSCAR: Do you know what people say about you? What they think about Ernesto? What people in the cooperative say about him?

ADELITA: I don't care to know.

OSCAR: If people keep on talking about you I'll have to get rid of Ernesto. This bus company is going to be a success—

ADELITA: We have two new buses, Oscar. We're doing very well.

OSCAR: We could have had the route to Regla, but people believe that my right hand and his wife should—

ADELITA: When they see you whoring in El Cañon, no one cares. No one repeats it.

OSCAR: You won't repeat it?

ADELITA: No, Oscar.

OSCAR: Neither will I. But don't go back. It's bad for the business, for our reputation.

ADELITA: Don't worry, if I see you coming, I'll hide.

Oscar goes back into the living room, he signals Mario, we can hear Adelita singing.

OSCAR: She's impossible.

MARIO: Yes.

OSCAR: We have to take care of it.

MARIO: Yes.

Oscar exits into the bedroom.

ARTURO: What were you discussing.

MARIO: Nothing.

ARTURO: I want a report of everything that goes on, with our company.

MARIO: It's Ernesto.

ARTURO: What about him.

MARIO: He cannot handle the job.

ARTURO: That's not true, he's a good worker.

MARIO: The other partners in the cooperative won't deal with him. They do all the business with Oscar, Oscar makes all the arrangements about financing, the routes we'll get, everything. They won't deal with Ernesto.

ARTURO: Why won't they?

MARIO: They say he's too shy.

MIGUEL: He has no balls, Papa! I hate to say it, he's my brother but he has no real balls!

ARTURO: Shut up, Miguel! (*He hits Miguel*)

MARIO: Miguel's right, anybody who stays at home while his wife goes to bars with other guys. What man could respect a man like that. And they don't want business dealings with him, they don't trust him.

ARTURO: They're going to have to. I'll deal with Ernesto.

Mario and Miguel start to exit to their rooms.

Where are you going?

MARIO: To get dressed, Papa. Get ready for the town.

MIGUEL: Some excitement, Papa!

ARTURO: That's right, show them, show them for your father.

MARIO: You're a legend, Papa.

ARTURO: That's true, I am. It comes from running around in the mountains fighting Spaniards. It gives you courage—

Mario and Miguel exit. Arturo pours himself another drink. In the bedroom, Manuela is asleep, Oscar is getting dressed. Manuela wakes up.

MANUELA: Oscar, come here. Oscar, don't leave. Oscar, sit next to me. My grandmother was just in this room with my little brother, Enrique. She told me she wanted me and my baby, that I had been chosen to go with them.

OSCAR: Oh, sweetie, a nightmare.

MANUELA: I said, "Oh, please, not my baby, not me. I can't go now. I'm too happy."

OSCAR: I'm glad she didn't take you.

MANUELA: She gestured "Fine," and walked away. My little brother said, "But we need a family member. Remember?" Then they walked away. Don't go out. Stay with me. Hold me, caress me, Oscar.

OSCAR: You're pregnant.

MANUELA: It doesn't matter.

OSCAR: You'd get hurt. I couldn't take a chance then hurt you. What if the baby felt it, and it was born perverted? I couldn't take that risk. We shouldn't take the risk.

MANUELA: I need you.

THE MODERN LADIES OF GUANABACOA

OSCAR: I'm here.

MANUELA: I need you close. I'm shaking.

OSCAR: It was a nightmare.

MANUELA: No!

OSCAR: It's getting late.

MANUELA: Don't go away.

OSCAR: I have to.

MANUELA: Don't.

OSCAR: I'm late. Don't worry. The baby won't die.

MANUELA: Someone will.

OSCAR: I have to get dressed.

MANUELA: Let me watch while you get dressed. I like looking at your feet.

OSCAR: Why would anybody be interested in my feet? I have five toes, nothing special; nothing hard to figure out, right, I'm not complicated.

MANUELA: And I'm glad.

OSCAR: I know what I want. It's easy. Life is easy. You just have to make sure you win, that's all. Nothing else to it, dear. If I have a fever, I drink a shot of brandy; for headache a whiskey. An orphanage—that was the only thing I ever feared—but they didn't put me in one. I took care of myself. Here, do the cufflinks.

MANUELA: You're handsome, you know.

OSCAR: I'm never disappointed. I'll own the mansion up the street one day. That's what I want; that's what I'll get. I get everything I want.

MANUELA: You have me.

OSCAR: I don't worry. Ernesto is always worried, his nerves, his blood pressure, his toe hurts. Jesus, that's why Adelita goes looking...

MANUELA: My brother's delicate...

OSCAR: He's a coward. An affair, that's what he needs, with someone who'll slap him around a couple of times.

MANUELA: Don't be cruel.

OSCAR: That would reveal something to him. He'd know he was a coward and maybe start looking for his balls.

MANUELA: Stop talking about my brother that way.

OSCAR: Get me a glass of water. My mouth is dry from all this talking. Go and get it. Go, go, go.

He hands her the glass. He gives her little kisses. She smiles and goes to the dining room. Arturo is sitting in the dining room drinking brandy. Manuela pours a glass of water.

ARTURO: I once knew a little girl who sang to only me.

MANUELA: That was a long time ago, Papa. (*She blows him a kiss, walks to her room*)

ARTURO: I can still walk on water. (*He drinks more brandy*)

Manuela enters the bedroom.

MANUELA: Here, dear.

Oscar drinks the water.

OSCAR: Manuela, sit, listen, I'll have to decide soon if your brother is worth his share. I keep him because he is your brother. I feel obligated, because I love you. I'm in the family now. What a family. Quite a family, bunch of infants, your brothers.

MANUELA: You don't think I'm a coward?

OSCAR: No.

MANUELA: I love you.

OSCAR: Time to go.

MANUELA: No. A few more minutes. Until I fall back asleep.

She goes back to bed, Oscar watches her. Miguel enters the living room.

MIGUEL: Papa, time for work.

Arturo exits, Ernesto enters the living room from the kitchen.

ERNESTO: Miguel, you added up the money wrong again last night.

MIGUEL: I was short. That's impossible.

ERNESTO: You were over.

MIGUEL: What a pleasant surprise.

ERNESTO: You don't pay attention when you're adding. You're not careful.

MIGUEL: I was in a hurry.

ERNESTO: You're always in a hurry. Be careful. If not, we'll have to do it together. I won't be able to trust you.

MIGUEL: You're going to teach me?

ERNESTO: If I have to.

Adelita starts to sing.

MIGUEL: I'll wait for the lesson.

ERNESTO: Don't be angry.

MIGUEL: I'm not.

THE MODERN LADIES OF GUANABACOA

Miguel enters the porch, Ernesto exits to the kitchen.

Good evening.

ADELITA: Daydreaming again.

MIGUEL: Wonderful dreams.

ADELITA: Hmmm, me too.

MIGUEL: I dreamed about the airplane.

ADELITA: That you invented it, or that you flew in it?

MIGUEL: Please. (*He grabs Adelita's hand*)

ADELITA: Your brother is in the kitchen eating cake.

MIGUEL: Don't mention him.

ADELITA: You are not good.

MIGUEL: I'm not like Ernesto. Lunch tomorrow, at your house?

ADELITA: No. (*She hits him with her fan*) Tomorrow? I'll let you know. No. I'm sorry, I can't.

Miguel exits to the street. Adelita enters the living room. Maria Josefa and Ernesto enter from the kitchen. Ernesto is eating cake. Maria Josefa holds a cup of café with milk for him.

ERNESTO: Oscar's business ideas sure are good; one bus then two and so on. He says, "More tourists, more public transportation." Anyway, then he's thinking of hotels.

MARIA JOSEFA: More café, with milk, dear?

ERNESTO: No, Mama, water. And Adelita will get it.

MARIA JOSEFA: It's all right, Adelita. I'll get the water.

ADELITA: Fine.

ERNESTO: No, not fine, my mother's worked hard enough. Now it's my wife's turn.

ADELITA: She wants to do it.

ERNESTO: Let's not argue in front of my mother, please do it.

ADELITA: All right, water.

MARIA JOSEFA: Do you want another piece of cake? Wait, Adelita.

ERNESTO: Just water.

MARIA JOSEFA: Why? You didn't like it? I didn't put enough sugar, or did I put too much vanilla? Or is it the syrup, too much rum?

ERNESTO: Mama, my stomach hurts.

MARIA JOSEFA: Oh, I see.

ADELITA: Then just water? (*She smiles*)

ERNESTO: Yes. Just water, nothing else.

Adelita goes to the kitchen.

MARIA JOSEFA: Have you been eating at home?

ERNESTO: Sure, where else?

MARIA JOSEFA: Don't eat there, please. You know about her family and witch-craft. She would prefer if you were drugged.

ERNESTO: I have to trust her.

MARIA JOSEFA: No, you don't and—

ERNESTO: Oscar's other idea is sandwich shops all along the main highway with gasoline pumps.

MARIA JOSEFA: You shouldn't protect her; adultery...

ERNESTO: Adultery. You even know, even my mother knows.

Adelita enters. She hands him a glass.

ADELITA: Water.

MARIA JOSEFA: Without a plate. I'll bring a plate. (*She takes glass from Ernesto*) My son gets served with a plate.

ADELITA: Yes, Maria, of course, Maria Josefa, your son.

Maria Josefa exits.

ERNESTO: Respect my mother, at least my mother.

ADELITA: I'm a mother. Your son's mother.

ERNESTO: That's the only reason I haven't beaten you to a pulp...no one in this town would stop me, adulteress.

ADELITA: Adulteress, yes adultery. Your accusation, I know. I'm so bored with you.

Maria Josefa enters.

MARIA JOSEFA: Water, son. (*She hands him a glass with plate*)

ERNESTO: Thank you, Mama. (*He drinks, hands glass and plate back to her*)

MARIA JOSEFA: I'll take care of you. You and my grandson will live here, with me.

ADELITA: My son lives with me, you can have your son. If Ernesto had any courage, he'd be the one in charge.

MARIA JOSEFA: Adelita, what do you know about business?

ADELITA: Your husband's business is widely known.

MARIA JOSEFA: God forgives it in men, never in women. It will be hell for you.

ADELITA: And you, do you forgive?

MARIA JOSEFA: I don't forgive.

ADELITA: You are immune. Lucky you in heaven with a harp. Stop looking at me.

ERNESTO: I am looking for the truth.

ADELITA: You know the truth.

ERNESTO: I'm trying to see if there's anything good.

ADELITA: You had your chance.

ERNESTO: Damn you!

ADELITA: Weakling.

MARIA JOSEFA: Stop it.

ADELITA: Oscar's slave!

ERNESTO: Not in front of my mother.

ADELITA: Be a man, weakling.

MARIA JOSEFA: Get out.

ADELITA: You know the truth.

ERNESTO: Liar, it's till death do you part, Adelita.

Adelita goes to the porch.

I'm sorry, Mama. I'm sorry you had to see the fight. I'm sorry.

MARIA JOSEFA: I know, dear. I'm sorry, too.

Arturo enters in work clothes.

ARTURO: Ernesto, come with me for a drink, before I go to work.

ERNESTO: No.

ARTURO: Ernesto, you should spend less time with your mother and more time making your wife happy.

ERNESTO: You have to prove yourself, don't you?

ARTURO: Prove myself, no.

ERNESTO: You have to think you're the best?

ARTURO: No.

ERNESTO: You have to prove yourself with every woman.

ARTURO: No. Maria, go in the kitchen, I want a piece of cake.

MARIA JOSEFA: You don't need to protect me.

ARTURO: Maria, please go.

Maria Josefa lights a cigarette and begins to smoke it.

ERNESTO: Why don't I feel it, why doesn't my flesh feel it?

ARTURO: I don't know. Maybe I didn't do the right thing.

ERNESTO: What?

ARTURO: I should have bought you someone on your fifteenth birthday. I should have taken you to a whorehouse.

ERNESTO: You should have, she cuts off my balls. She takes my guts out. I'm everybody's fool. I don't want to think about it, but it's all I think about. That I'm betrayed, that I'm made fun of. I wanted all the good things. I wanted to be like Joseph was to Mary.

ARTURO: Leave her.

ERNESTO: I'd rather go to whores than go to her.

ARTURO: Then go to whores.

ERNESTO: I hope she dies.

ARTURO: Forget her. You need to be there with Oscar making all the decisions. I want you to represent us, to represent me. We own the bus company. Not just Oscar.

ERNESTO: Do you think witchcraft works?

ARTURO: Poison does.

ERNESTO: Hmmm. You'll be proud of me. Don't worry, Papa, I'll be in charge. I need another piece of cake.

MARIA JOSEFA: How big?

ERNESTO: No, Mama, you rest, I'll get it myself. (*He goes into the kitchen*)

MARIA JOSEFA: I'll be asleep, don't wake me; be quiet when you walk in. Don't put the sheets off me in the middle of the night.

ARTURO: Yes, fine. (*Pause*) And you leave Ernesto alone.

MARIA JOSEFA: He is mine, my son.

ARTURO: You feed him too much—

MARIA JOSEFA: He's pleasantly plump, he looks handsome that way. I have to take care of him. I have to be kind to him.

ARTURO: He has a wife!

MARIA JOSEFA: She's the image of you.

ARTURO: I am everything a husband is supposed to be. I provide. My business provided the money for this new enterprise. It is still my gamble. I am still the one in control. So stop stuffing my son with lies about me.

MARIA JOSEFA: I never turned him against you. You're his father. I tell all of them to love you. I know we all have weaknesses. I know what a wife, a mother is supposed to do. . .

ARTURO: Desire cannot be controlled. I am not expected to control that. And you—

THE MODERN LADIES OF GUANABACOA

MARIA JOSEFA: And I stop you? Do I? Arturo?!

ARTURO: You're a good woman.

MARIA JOSEFA: Decent?!

ARTURO: Yes, Maria Josefa. Decent.

Ernesto enters eating cake.

How many pieces today?

ERNESTO: This is the third piece, I think. Oh sweets, Mama makes the best cake, better than any bakery.

ARTURO: Think about what I told you.

ERNESTO: Yes, I will.

ARTURO: Time to get to work.

Arturo kisses Maria Josefa lightly on the forehead.

MARIA JOSEFA: Till tomorrow. In the morning I won't wake you.

ARTURO: Fine, Maria.

Arturo goes to the porch, Adelita looks at him.

ERNESTO: I'll bring you café later.

MARIA JOSEFA: Do you love him?

ERNESTO: Yes, Mama, I love both of you, you gave me everything.

Arturo and Adelita are on the porch.

ARTURO: Adelita, you're a marvel, you get lovelier every year, instead of older.

ADELITA: Maybe I'll divorce him.

ARTURO: I'll divorce Maria if you do.

ADELITA: And we'll live happily ever after?

ARTURO: For a few minutes at least.

ADELITA: They'll burn us at the stake.

ARTURO: We'll keep it to ourselves, don't let anyone know anything you do in this town.

ADELITA: Yes.

ARTURO: You would be worth it.

ADELITA: Thank you.

Blackout. Lights up on Mario and Oscar entering the living room.

OSCAR: What can I do?

MARIO: Do what you have to do, you have to do it, do it.

OSCAR: Would you?

MARIO: For the good of the business?

OSCAR: Yes.

MARIO: I'd do anything for the good of the business.

OSCAR: I'm going to give Ernesto another chance.

MARIO: Another chance.

OSCAR: One, one more chance.

MARIO: And if it's hopeless?

OSCAR: You'll be second in command.

MARIO: Thank you.

OSCAR: Ernesto will feel defeated.

MARIO: I'll reconcile with my brother.

OSCAR: Will you be able to take care of that?

MARIO: Are you kidding, I'm the one who sweats in ice and is cool in the middle of a fire.

Adelita sings "Tea for Two."

OSCAR: Tell him another week.

MARIO: I will, have a good time.

OSCAR: I will.

Oscar exits to the street. Mario crosses to the porch.

MARIO: Ernesto.

ERNESTO: Mario.

MARIO: I'm out on the porch.

ERNESTO: A minute.

Adelita is singing.

MARIO: The singing parrot.

ADELITA: Who?

MARIO: You. You are the singing parrot.

ADELITA: I have a good voice. (*Sings*) "Nobody near us to see us or hear us. No friends or relations on weekend vacations." It's nice to listen to. Sounds respectable.

MARIO: Respectable?!

ADELITA: I have a respectable voice. It doesn't crack.

MARIO: That's true, it doesn't crack, but it's not great. People wouldn't pay to hear it.

THE MODERN LADIES OF GUANABACOA

ADELITA: I'm not asking anyone to pay.

MARIO: Then why do it, Adelita?

ADELITA: To entertain myself, Mario. To amuse myself, to hear myself.

Ernesto enters.

MARIO: Ernesto, Oscar asked my advice. I stood by you, you know that.

ERNESTO: Thank you.

MARIO: Oscar told me to tell you, you have one more week.

ERNESTO: A week? What do I do wrong? I work hard. Why are you all so concerned?

MARIO: You're not pushy. You're not aggressive.

ERNESTO: I do my job.

MARIO: Oscar has to do all the bargaining, make all the deals so we have good routes. If you are second in command you have to wheel and deal, get other people to trust you. To believe in you. You have to have the kind of reputation people can believe in.

ERNESTO: Only Oscar can do that.

MARIO: No...

ADELITA: Can you wheel and deal?

MARIO: Absolutely. Yes I can.

ADELITA: Lucky you.

Miguel enters.

MIGUEL: Papa got shot! Papa was shot!

ERNESTO: Shot! Shot! Shot!

ADELITA: Why? WHY?

MARIO: He was at the bus yard?

MIGUEL: Oscar's with him now. He wants you, Mario.

ADELITA: Arturo, Arturo? Arturo?...Ernesto.

MIGUEL: Ernesto, he's dying.

ERNESTO: My father is dying. My father?

Maria Josefa stands in the front door and listens to them talk.

ADELITA: Who shot him?

MIGUEL: It must have been Beatrice's husband. Papa was walking down the street, Beatrice's husband must have followed him down the block, it happened in front of the bus yard. He must have heard about Beatrice and Papa. He shot Papa in the back.

MARIO: Beatrice the American?

MARIA JOSEFA: Beatrice, the adulteress. Beatrice the cheat. Beatrice, the fraud. He got shot because of her. Don't forget. He who was never going to bring it home. Who kept it discreet. Where's Manuela?

MARIO: In her room.

MARIA JOSEFA: Good, I don't want her to know about that American.

MARIO: You're right, Mama. She's his daughter, she must be protected.

MARIA JOSEFA: Is he going to be all right?

MARIO: Yes, Mama. He'll be fine.

MARIA JOSEFA: I'll stay here with Manuela.

MIGUEL: Oscar wants Mario to go.

MARIA JOSEFA: Did anyone see it happen?

MIGUEL: No, Oscar found him on the ground.

MARIA JOSEFA: Good. We'll keep it our secret.

MARIO: Of course.

Maria Josefa and Ernesto enter the living room.

MARIA JOSEFA: I spend my life with him looking at me. He made me feel wanted once. Ernesto, you go too, come back and get me when the doctors are through with him. You should be with him. Go be a good son.

Ernesto starts to walk out. Adelita follows him.

ERNESTO: You stay here and pray.

Blackout. Lights up. Maria Josefa kneeling with her rosary. Long pause.

MARIA JOSEFA: I can't remember one prayer.

Manuela enters.

MANUELA: Where is everyone?

MARIA JOSEFA: Your father had a little accident. Don't worry, he'll be fine.

MANUELA: What kind of accident?

MARIA JOSEFA: He was shot in the arm.

MANUELA: Shot?

MARIA JOSEFA: Help me remember the prayer.

MANUELA: In the name of the Father and of the Son . . .

MARIA JOSEFA: Now I remember.

MANUELA: Oh.

THE MODERN LADIES OF GUANABACOA

MARIA JOSEFA: What's wrong?

MANUELA: The baby kicked.

MARIA JOSEFA: He's telling us to pray.

MANUELA: She does it all the time.

MARIA JOSEFA: That means he's strong.

Adelita enters.

ADELITA: Here are the candles. I'll light them.

MARIA JOSEFA: Learn from his mistakes. Learn from it, Adelita.

MANUELA: Did they rob him?

MARIA JOSEFA: Let's pray.

MANUELA: Where were we?

MARIA JOSEFA: Another Hail Mary.

*All three kneel and pray silently and quickly. Mechanically they do
a Hail Mary.*

MARIA JOSEFA, MANUELA, ADELITA: Hail Mary full of grace, the Lord is with
thee. Blessed art thou among women and blessed is the fruit of thy
womb, Jesus. Holy Mary mother of God, pray for us sinners now and
at the hour of our death, amen.

MANUELA: We should go and be with him.

ADELITA: I think so. Let's go.

MARIA JOSEFA: No. They'll probably bring him home in a little while.

MANUELA: Are you sure he's not hurt?

MARIA JOSEFA: It's nothing serious, pray.

ADELITA: I don't know, Maria.

MARIA JOSEFA: Adelita, he was shot in the arm, a surface wound, that's all.

MANUELA: Maybe they lied to you?

MARIA JOSEFA: Of course not.

MANUELA: Everything scares me. He'll be safe?

MARIA JOSEFA: Yes, I'm sure.

MANUELA: You promise me?

MARIA JOSEFA: I promise, dear. It's just a small wound, nothing to worry
about.

ADELITA: Not in the arm, Maria—

MARIA JOSEFA: In the arm, Adelita! Remember. Is the baby calmer?

MANUELA: No.

ADELITA: Oh.

MARIA JOSEFA: Still moving around?

MANUELA: Yes.

ADELITA: They do that a lot.

MANUELA: Not as much as today.

MARIA JOSEFA: He's getting ready.

MANUELA: Maybe she will come today, maybe today will be her birthday.

MARIA JOSEFA: Pray, girls, time to pray.

All three pray silently and quickly; mechanically they do three Hail Marys. Ernesto and Miguel enter.

MIGUEL: Mama, he's asking for you. We came to get you.

MARIA JOSEFA: How is he?

MIGUEL: Fine, Mama, fine.

MARIA JOSEFA: For once he'll have to listen. He'll hate it. He hates to be told what to do. Basques are like that. That's why the Spaniards kicked them out. The Spaniards told them what they were supposed to do, but they were always rebelling. They called themselves something peculiar. . . (*She thinks*) "Anarchists." So the Spanish threw them out. He has books about it in our bedroom. We should burn them. We shouldn't have books like that around us. I don't think he even believed in Baby Jesus. He was wild.

MIGUEL: He had balls.

MARIA JOSEFA: Build businesses. Now it's up to the two of you.

ERNESTO: You're right, Mama.

MARIA JOSEFA: It's time to face him. Manuela, you stay here.

MANUELA: Why?

MARIA JOSEFA: He is in a hospital. You don't want to catch a disease. Continue the rosary while you wait.

MANUELA: Tell him I love him. Adelita, will you stay with me?

ADELITA: Yes.

The rest exit. Manuela kneels and then Adelita kneels.

What prayer were we up to?

MANUELA: The fifth Hail Mary.

ADELITA: Thirty-five more to go.

MANUELA: Maybe we were up to the middle of Our Father. I never know what I'm up to when I do the rosary. Maybe the seventh Hail Mary?

Maybe we should start from the beginning. I think it's a sin if you pick it up in the middle. Do you remember the rules, Adelita?

ADELITA: No, I forget. We better make sure we're doing it the right way.

MANUELA: Let's begin at the beginning. In the name of the Father and of the Son. . . . Oh. She's been kicking all afternoon. Isn't it odd, a baby is such a saintly thing, and the act of making him or her makes one feel so wicked.

ADELITA: You feel wicked?

MANUELA: Yes, I'm not Papa's good girl anymore. (*She cries*)

ADELITA: Your father is a hypocrite.

MANUELA: Don't speak about Papa that way. My father is strict, proper, and moral.

ADELITA: To impress you.

MANUELA: You want to put everyone in the soup you're in.

ADELITA: I flirt. That's all.

MANUELA: Please stop your lies.

ADELITA: They are lying to you. Your father was with Beatrice. The American. Her husband. . .shot Arturo in the back because of adultery. Because of sex.

MANUELA: You are lying. I do not believe you.

ADELITA: Even your mother knows.

MANUELA: I'll pull your hair and kick your teeth in, slut.

Adelita slaps Manuela. Manuela slaps her back.

ADELITA: It's not fair, you're pregnant. I can't hurt you. Let's stop.

MANUELA: All right. I'll stop for the baby, I'll stop. (*She kneels*) In the name of the. . .

ADELITA: Manuela. . .

MANUELA: Let me pray.

ADELITA: Why am I not allowed to talk in this house? Why don't you consider me a part of the life here in this family? I get tolerated, that's all. . .

MANUELA: Hail Mary full of—

ADELITA: I've been the burden you all struggle with, your family's embarrassment.

MANUELA: Please stop, I don't want to hear anymore.

ADELITA: Beatrice's husband found your father, he searched for your father. He shot and the shot succeeded. They're lying to you to keep you in line. Your father is dying.

MANUELA: Get out, Adelita.

ADELITA: If Ernesto wants me, I'm at my mother's, with his baby. (*She exits to the porch*)

MANUELA: My father is dying. (*She cries. She reads from a prayer book*)

Oscar walks onto the back porch, sees Adelita.

"The Lord created man out of earth and turns him back to it again. He gave men a few days, a limited time."

ADELITA: I told her about Beatrice and Arturo. She knows...

OSCAR: Tell me why, Adelita? Tell me.

MANUELA: "He made him tongue and eyes and a mind for thinking."

ADELITA: She should know that the men in this town are cheats and liars and a bunch of hypocrites...

OSCAR: I could say that about a few of the women...

ADELITA: No. The women in this town pretend, they pretend to each other that nothing is going on...

MANUELA: "He filled him with knowledge and understanding, and showed him good and evil..." (*She touches her stomach*)

ADELITA: ... then we accuse each other. But with you men we are taught to look the other way and forgive and smile. (*She smiles at Oscar*)

OSCAR: You are a whore.

MANUELA: "...and showed him the majesty of his work..."

ADELITA: I am a saint compared to you men. You know that. You know what everybody is doing.

Adelita exits. Oscar enters the living room. Manuela cries in his arms.

OSCAR: My darling, sweetie, my china doll. I'll take care of you, my piece of caramel.

MANUELA: You do love me?

OSCAR: Yes. On my mother's grave.

MANUELA: And the first time you look at a woman and you want her, tell me so I'm not blind.

OSCAR: That'll never happen.

MANUELA: But if it happens, you'll tell me, promise me. I'm not a coward. I have to be the only one in your thoughts every second, and if it ever stops, I want to know.

OSCAR: You are always in my thoughts. Every time I look at a passenger getting in the bus, I think, another dime for Manuela and what she has inside.

MANUELA: If you ever touch someone else—I could never let go if it wasn't you—oh, it kicked again. (*She laughs*)

OSCAR: Can I put my hand and feel it? (*He does*) What should we name him?

MANUELA: After my father, Arturo. (*She cries*) I loved him.

OSCAR: And if it's a girl, Manuela.

MANUELA: No, I hate my name.

OSCAR: Carmen.

MANUELA: No, this horrible woman I knew was named Carmen. I could never call my baby that.

OSCAR: Tamara.

MANUELA: That sounds like a tango dancer.

OSCAR: Dun, dun dun dun, tra la la la la.

They start to tango.

And she'll be able to tango and waltz.

MANUELA: How refined. (*She laughs*)

OSCAR: And never worry, because what's inside you, the baby Tamara, Arturo, Carmen—

MANUELA: Sonia?

OSCAR: Sonia, yes, Sonia is going to look like a millionaire.

MANUELA: And you'll want me only till we're dust.

OSCAR: Someday, I'll buy cars and boats and go on vacations to Spain for you.

MANUELA: If it ever changes tell me. You're the only person I respect.

OSCAR: I will work only for you, struggle for you and cheat people for you. You, my family.

MANUELA: Yes, our family, you and me and what's inside of me.

OSCAR: We'll put your brothers on salary, not shares but regular salaries.

MANUELA: If you think it's best.

OSCAR: It's a unique concept, but it assures perfect results.

MANUELA: If you think it's right...

OSCAR: In business you must blend meticulously all the ingredients. Number one, the boss equals the owners; number two, then there are the workers; if you have these two things clearly defined, it'll work one hundred percent of the time. In any type of business.... It's the way they blend café...

MANUELA: Kahwah. (*She laughs*)

OSCAR: The right beans together make black gold, for white gods.

Maria Josefa and Mario enter.

MARIO: Oscar, you're safe, you're here.

MARIA JOSEFA: Manuela, I have to talk to Oscar. I need a few moments with Oscar.

MANUELA: Mama, I want to know everything that goes on!

OSCAR: Yes, Maria Josefa?

MARIO: He's dead. Papa is dead!

Mario starts to cry. Oscar helps Manuela onto a chair, she is also crying.

OSCAR: Have they found Beatrice's husband?!

MARIA JOSEFA: It was not Beatrice's husband.

MANUELA: Stop lying, I know.

MARIA JOSEFA: What do you know?

MANUELA: Adelita told me the truth.

MARIA JOSEFA: It was the capital warning us. It was a threat. One of President Machado's men came up to me. He stood next to me while they were taking your father's body away. And whispered: "This is only the beginning, tell your group to get wise."

OSCAR: But . . . . They've been taken care of. The cooperative took care of that!

MARIO: But they want it all, they want the rest of us to be slaves . . . just like Papa said.

MARIA JOSEFA: We won't let them. You and I cannot let them, Oscar. We have to advance.

OSCAR: Of course, that's what Arturo wanted. Mario, when we are in control we'll slit their throats, one after the other, like at a chicken farm.

MARIO: Is that what Father wanted?

MANUELA: Yes!

MARIO: Here's the money.

OSCAR: Good.

MARIO: No one stole anything. Are they going to kill us all!!

OSCAR: I will not live in poverty. I will not be a pauper; and my children will only see wealth . . . we'll pretend they didn't say it.

MARIA JOSEFA: Yes!

OSCAR: Maria Josefa, her husband killed him, domestic.

MARIA JOSEFA: That's right.

OSCAR: But we'll be on the lookout. On our guard.

MARIO: No, there has to be some kind of justice.

OSCAR: The only justice is capital.

MARIO: They have to pay.

OSCAR: Who killed your husband, Maria Josefa?

MARIA JOSEFA: A jealous husband.

MANUELA: That's right, Mario. It was Beatrice's husband, it wasn't politics. He probably sent that other man there to start a rumor to cover up his act. It was Beatrice that killed Papa.

MARIA JOSEFA: Mario, your father was killed by?

MARIO: No, please Mama.

OSCAR: Your father was killed by a . . .

Pause.

MARIO: By a woman's lust and betrayal.

OSCAR: Give me the money. I'll count the money, you mourn.

Mario hands Oscar money.

MARIA JOSEFA: Yes. Go be with your father. Dress him in his white suit.

Mario exits.

OSCAR: You ladies go dress in black, I'll take care of business.

MARIA JOSEFA: No, Manuela will count the money, she's the best at mathematics. Manuela will count the money from now on.

MANUELA: Why?

MARIA JOSEFA: You represent both of us, both our interests.

Oscar hands Manuela the money.

OSCAR: China doll, count.

He touches her and then exits. Manuela starts to count the money.

MARIA JOSEFA: Do a good job, suppress your feelings and work. Be in control. That's why we cut our hair.

MANUELA: We will be happy, Oscar and me.

MARIA JOSEFA: That will be my prayer, that you're the lucky one, the one that doesn't have to keep it all inside, all a secret.

MANUELA: This is for her, Mama. She'll be able to afford to be arrogant.

MARIA JOSEFA: She won't be dishonored like me.

MANUELA: Oscar will buy it all for her.

MARIA JOSEFA: No. We will buy it all for her.

MANUELA: Feel, Mama, she's kicking hard. She'll make you happy. Sonia, Sonia Luz Hernandez.

MARIA JOSEFA: Ripoll.

MANUELA: I have to ask Oscar where to hide the money. (*She starts to exit*)

MARIA JOSEFA: Let me know where he hides it.

MANUELA: Yes.

Manuela exits. Maria Josefa lights a cigarette.

MARIA JOSEFA: Arturo the Basque and Maria Josefa... (*She smokes*) Arturo, who won? Maria Josefa. Because, Maria Josefa is alive. (*She smokes*)

Blackout.

END OF PLAY

FABIOLA

CHARACTERS

The ages are the characters' ages at the start of the play, in 1955.

CUSA, the lady of the house, in her forties
PEDRO, her son, Fabiola's widower, early twenties
OSVALDO, Pedro's brother, in his twenties
MIRIAM, their sister, seventeen
SONIA HERNANDEZ, Osvaldo's wife, twenty-five
CLARA, Cusa's other daughter-in-law, twenty-two
ALFREDO, Cusa's husband, a tyrant, fifty
RAULITO, a nice boy, nineteen
OCTAVIO, Fabiola's cousin
CONCHITA, a maid, fifty
MILICIANO 1, thirty, handsome
MILICIANO 2

TIME

Act One, Scene 1: 1955
Act One, Scene 2: 1959
Act Two, Scenes 1–3: 1961
Act Two, Scene 4: 1967

PLACE

A nineteenth-century Spanish mansion in Guanabacoa, Cuba.

FABIOLA

ACT ONE

A nineteenth-century Spanish mansion in Guanabacoa, Cuba, a beach town near Havana. A ballroom, a kitchen, an upstairs room.

The ballroom has many windows, a door leading to the outside, two doors leading to a porch that surrounds the ballroom, and an entranceway with marble columns leading to the rest of the house. The room is designed for dancing: there are chairs, a baby grand piano, a record player and a coffee table stacked with records.

The large kitchen has a Spanish tile floor, a twelve-burner stove, two ovens and a long high counter with ten stools. Down right is a radio and a large refrigerator. A spiral staircase leads to the upper room.

The upper room, decorated in the style of the 1930s, has a mirrored closet the size of one wall, stage left and visible above the kitchen. The room is done in shades of peach or pink. There is a large bed, a window, a door leading to a bathroom with a large tub, and a door to the spiral staircase. The window curtains are completely closed.

Scene 1

The ballroom on a hot August day. All the lights are off except for candles lit in front of a statue of Saint Barbara sitting atop the baby grand piano. She is surrounded by many food offerings. In the center of the large ballroom are Sonia, Osvaldo, Pedro, Miriam, Cusa, Clara and Raulito. They are sitting in a circle, praying.

ALL: We implore you Almighty God to send only good spirits, and to send away all the evil spirits who may guide us toward sin. Give us the light to distinguish truth from lies, send away all evil spirits who reincarnated would lead us away from love and charity toward our neighbors, and if any of them should appear don't let them possess any of us.

Pause.

SONIA: Fabiola?. . . Play the piano for us. . .anything. . .

CUSA: You're not doing it right. I told you we should hire a professional.

MIRIAM: You do it, Mama. God knows you spend enough time on curses.

CUSA: But I hire the right people to help me.

OSVALDO: Stop fighting and start praying.

They pray.

CUSA: You're right. Only God can help her and us now.

Cusa lights a cigar and they pass it around as they pray.

Saint Barbara, bring her back to us: Fabiola and my sweet dead grandson.

CLARA: You have sweet live ones too. Sonia and I made sure of that.

SONIA: Stop thinking about your position in the family and try to help her.

They pray.

CLARA: Cousin Fabiola, help me to endure this life.

MIRIAM: No, Clara. We're supposed to help her get to heaven; you're not supposed to ask anything of her. No wonder she won't come back down.

SONIA: Have faith. All of us need faith.

OSVALDO: Yes, Fabiola, we who are still alive loved you, but you disappeared; your body has disappeared. They don't know what mausoleum they've put you in. You were supposed to be in your father's mausoleum, but when they went to bury your great-uncle Federico, your casket was gone. Why did you do this to us? Draw us a map and tell us where you are. . . . Come to me, Fabiola. Pedro wants you too.

SONIA: Help us.

They all sit silent for a minute.

PEDRO: Nothing. You want nothing from me; she doesn't even want me to help you find her. (*Pause*) There's nothing. This is all crap. Let's stop.

He turns on the lights; they all react to the change in lighting.

CUSA: I'm sorry, but tomorrow I'm hiring somebody who makes a living at doing this kind of thing.

PEDRO: Why, Mama? There's nothing to contact. There's nothing left of her; even her remains were stolen.

SONIA: No, there is heaven; she's somewhere between heaven and hell!

MIRIAM: Then she must be here in Cuba!

CUSA: I'll call a gypsy tomorrow.

PEDRO: No, it's over.

CUSA: It won't be over till we bury her in the right place.

PEDRO: It's over! I don't want anyone to know about it but us. I don't want anyone to know that I lost her.

CUSA: Pour yourself a drink, and relax.

PEDRO: I don't want to relax! I want to have you watch me while I burn, while my brain dissolves in front of your eyes. I want all of you to see the destruction.

MIRIAM: He's been drinking.

OSVALDO: Since early this morning.

Pause.

MIRIAM: Should we get him another?

OSVALDO: Sure, till we all pass out. (*Pause*) I'll go to the kitchen and get wine. (*He exits*)

RAULITO: Where's your father?

Pause.

MIRIAM: Not here.

RAULITO: I can see that.

MIRIAM: Good. You have eyes.

Pause.

PEDRO: Miriam, play a record.

MIRIAM: What?

PEDRO: Something American.

Miriam puts on a record: Nat King Cole singing "Unforgettable." Off-stage, Osvaldo screams. Enter Osvaldo, shaking with fear. The front of his shirt is wet with red wine.

OSVALDO: She was here! I just saw her!

PEDRO: What did she tell you?

OSVALDO: She kissed me.

SONIA: Well, you told her you loved her!

PEDRO: How did it feel?

OSVALDO: I don't know. She told me to kiss you.

CLARA: Stop teasing.

RAULITO: You're putting us on, right?

OSVALDO: No. It's the truth. (*He starts to shake*) Can't you see that it's the truth?

CUSA: Show me where she was. (*She starts to exit*)

PEDRO: The truth, huh? Osvaldo, why did she come to you?

Osvaldo starts to exit.

Was the baby with her?

Exit Cusa.

OSVALDO: No, she looked the way she looked when I first saw her.

PEDRO: When we fell in love with her.

SONIA: When *you* fell in love with her!

Exit Osvaldo and Pedro. Pause.

CLARA: I want to see it too. (*She exits*)

RAULITO: Want to dance?

MIRIAM: Not now. I'll walk you home later.

RAULITO: I didn't want to get a feel.

MIRIAM: Too bad. I did.

SONIA: Wild.

MIRIAM: Who?

SONIA: You. If the nuns saw you now. They're having a breakfast next week. They're going to give Fabiola a mass. Isn't it bizarre, death? Isn't it uncanny that someone you know actually goes, and stops being there, and you wonder why it wasn't you!

MIRIAM: She's still alive. She gets more attention now than when she was alive.

SONIA: That kind of attention I don't want. Do you think we've done enough mourning?

MIRIAM: Plenty. You want to go shopping tomorrow?

SONIA: No, I want to go swimming.

MIRIAM: Maybe we should buy ourselves black swimsuits.

SONIA: Or we could go swimming at night.

MIRIAM: Wicked. Now who's the wicked girl?

RAULITO: No, the sharks come out at night.

MIRIAM: That's right.

Sonia starts to walk toward the kitchen, then turns.

SONIA: I'm walking over to my mother's! I want a snack! Papa bought some apples imported from Spain. He said they were delicious! And cheese!

MIRIAM: I'll go with you.

RAULITO: I'll watch over you.

SONIA: It's only across the street.

MIRIAM: He wants his feel now.

RAULITO: Miriam, show a little respect for my feelings!

They exit. Enter Osvaldo and Pedro.

PEDRO: Mama's going to build a shrine on the spot.

OSVALDO: I shouldn't have said anything; maybe it was a hallucination. Maybe she wasn't real at all.

PEDRO: Maybe you just wanted an excuse to kiss me.

OSVALDO: Oh, yes. That must be it.

PEDRO: Remember when we used to experiment?

OSVALDO: Quiet.

PEDRO: Didn't you enjoy it?

OSVALDO: I can't remember. I was young. You had just started shaving.

PEDRO: I enjoyed it. I know you did too. It lasted too long.

OSVALDO: Did you ever confess that to the priest?

PEDRO: Never. Did you?

OSVALDO: Of course not! Confessing masturbation was bad enough. Lectures and acts of contrition and Our Fathers. Can you imagine what would have happened if I'd told him that?

PEDRO: What?

OSVALDO: You know what. That.

PEDRO: That?

OSVALDO: Us.

PEDRO: Us that committed incest?

OSVALDO: We just helped each other. We just played with each other. Nothing to it.

PEDRO: Then why does it make you so nervous? She told you to kiss me. Follow the dead's orders.

THE FLOATING ISLAND PLAYS

Enter Conchita. She is holding a clean shirt. Sara follows.

CONCHITA: Here's a clean shirt. Your mother wants you to put it on right now.

OSVALDO: Give it to me. Unbutton it for me, will you? You know I don't like to unbutton my own shirts.

CONCHITA: Give it to me. You're such a baby. You have a baby and you act like a baby.

Sara is taking the statue of Saint Barbara from the top of the piano.

PEDRO: Don't do that.

SARA: Your mother wants it out in the hall now.

CONCHITA: At the site. If we want to reach her we have to pray at the correct site.

PEDRO: Like Lourdes. She'll save the cripples in this house.

CONCHITA: There are no cripples in this house.

SARA: Should I blow out the candles?

CONCHITA: No. Take the candles first. I'll follow you with Saint Barbara, but close your eyes while Mr. Osvaldo takes off his shirt.

SARA: I wouldn't be tempted.

CONCHITA: You never know.

PEDRO: But I might be tempted.

SARA: Respect me, please, sir.

PEDRO: I do. I do respect you. You don't suffer.

SARA: Thank you. I'm sorry about your wife. I liked her.

CONCHITA: I loved her, poor girl. But don't worry. We'll get her out of purgatory. His shirt, he unbuttoned his own dirty shirt. Close your eyes, Sara!

Sara covers her eyes. Osvaldo changes his shirt.

I'll button it for you.

OSVALDO: Why can you see my skin?

CONCHITA: 'Cause I gave you baths all your life. Don't get uppity with me!

SARA (*Her eyes still closed*): Why do you think that I don't suffer?

PEDRO: Because you work. You have tasks that you do. Enjoyable things like cooking and taking care of my nieces and nephews, playing with them, filling your days with little details that take up hours and weeks...

SARA: You could work too.

PEDRO: No.

SARA: Why not?

PEDRO: Because if I did something it would have to be something important.

SARA: Like what?

PEDRO: Like lead a revolution.

CONCHITA: All right. You can open your eyes. Put all the candles on the tray...and I'll carry Saint Barbara. We'll have a procession. That's the only way to deal with religious items. Treat them like the church treats them. Then you don't get into any trouble.

SARA: I'm ready.

CONCHITA: Let's go. Make the sign of the cross as I walk by, boys.

They don't.

Don't play with God. That's something that one should not play with. He knows what's in your mind.

Exit Conchita and Sara.

PEDRO: Where should we meet?

OSVALDO: Let's talk about it later.

PEDRO: But where? The garage?

OSVALDO: No, the chauffeur will hear us.

PEDRO: The chauffeur is with Dad. Dad won't be back from whoring till dawn. So, we're meeting there before dawn?

OSVALDO: No.

PEDRO: The honeymoon room?

Enter Clara.

CLARA: I tried to wake Ricardo up, I said there is a ghost in the house, the dead has come back from the grave.

OSVALDO: What did he say?

CLARA: "So what? I have to practice for basketball tomorrow." What dedication to a sport; I mean for an adult.

OSVALDO: It's good for him. But the difference between me and Ricardo is that he doesn't have enough energy and I have too much. I bet I'll beat him tomorrow.

CLARA: How much? Five dollars?

OSVALDO: All right.

PEDRO: Actually, the difference between us and our younger brother is that he's a dunce and we are not.

CLARA: I can't let you get away with that! Do you know what he thinks about you?

Enter Sara and Conchita.

PEDRO: Well, tell me.

CLARA: I don't discuss family matters in front of the servants. (*Pause*) Where are the girls?

SARA: I saw them walking toward Sonia's father's house.

CLARA: Thank you. And of course, they didn't invite me.

OSVALDO: You were trying to wake your husband, trying to get a rise from the dead.

CONCHITA: Clara, help me with the food.

CLARA: No.

CONCHITA: Cusa thinks it's important to carry all the offerings over at once.

CLARA: Then you figure out a way to do it.

CONCHITA: Just one dish.

CLARA: But my manicure. Why can't Cusa do it?

CONCHITA: Because she's the lady of the house.

Sonia enters eating an apple. She walks toward the kitchen.

CLARA: And what am I?

SARA: A girl that married smart.

Clara spits into Sara's face.

CLARA: I won't take that kind of talk from a servant.

SONIA: Then don't spit into anybody's face. Nobody wants your spit. If you want to be a lady, learn how to treat people, Clara. Learn how to treat them.

CONCHITA: Where's Miriam?!

SONIA: Outside.

CONCHITA: Without a chaperone. I'm going out there right now.

Exit Conchita. Enter Cusa.

CUSA: The offerings! Sonia, grab a dish, Clara, Sara. . . . And I'll take the tray. Place the offerings underneath Saint Barbara. And boys, bring in the flowers. And turn off the records. No records today.

FABIOLA

Exit Cusa, Sonia, Sara, Clara. Osvaldo turns off the record player.

PEDRO: Well?

OSVALDO: Well?

They exit. Enter Miriam. Her blouse is off.

MIRIAM: It's just my nipples; the rest is still intact.

Enter Conchita.

CONCHITA: You put me to shame.

MIRIAM: Why? I am not your daughter.

CONCHITA (*Helping Miriam put on her blouse*): But I raised you. He's a good boy. If you give him too much, he'll never marry you.

MIRIAM: Who cares? Tell him to come in. You're the one that's scaring him off.

CONCHITA: No.

MIRIAM: Yes.

CONCHITA: Come back in, Raulito.

MIRIAM: Apologize to him.

CONCHITA: It's not your fault. It's her fault. I know that a man cannot resist. It's up to the young lady. Behave.

Conchita exits. Enter Raulito.

RAULITO: Do you think she'll tell your mother?

MIRIAM: No.

RAULITO: Are you sure?

MIRIAM: Positive.

Miriam turns on record player. The record is Nat King Cole singing "Young at Heart."

RAULITO: How can you be?

MIRIAM: Because it's happened before.

RAULITO: Don't hurt me like that. I am the only one.

MIRIAM: Let's dance.

RAULITO: I am. I know I am. You just like to shock.

MIRIAM: Some day I'm going to figure a way out.

RAULITO: From what?

They dance. Enter Sonia. She is carrying a rosary.

SONIA: Go out into the hall. They're starting a rosary to her.

MIRIAM: I owe her that much. Let's go pray, Raulito.

RAULITO: I'll turn off the record player.

SONIA: No, that's all right. I'll do it. I don't want to go in there yet. Pedro is being mean.

RAULITO: To you?

SONIA: To everyone.

> *Exit Miriam and Raulito. Sonia goes to turn off the record player. Before she does, she sits at the piano and begins to shake. She closes her eyes. The record is at the end and stops automatically. She swoons.*

Is this a spiritual moment? Is this what being spiritual is all about?

> *Enter Osvaldo.*

OSVALDO: He's attacking me now. Who cares about him?

SONIA: I do. He's been in touch with real tragedy. Something devastating really happened to him.

OSVALDO: If it happened to him, it happened to the family.

SONIA: What's this the beginning of, Osvaldo? Before Fabiola died nothing bad had happened to me, nothing unkind even. My life was beautiful. I got married, have a beautiful baby, I'm pretty. My mother and father are alive. What is this the beginning of? Is this the beginning of getting old? Is that what this is? Is life over when things like this happen?

OSVALDO: No, we are young. Thirty is old, but not twenty.

SONIA: But she's gone; she was our age. She's dead. Lost. We can't even find her body. There's nothing left of her. What if we died? What would be left of us in the world?

OSVALDO: Oscar!

SONIA: He's only a baby. He wouldn't remember us.

OSVALDO: But he would be us.

SONIA: I don't want to end up alone like her, trying to reach people in this house. A moment ago Fabiola touched me.

OSVALDO: Why is she coming to us?

SONIA: Because she knows we'll help him. She knows we'd do anything for Pedro.

OSVALDO: Would you?

SONIA: Yes. You're my husband, he's your brother; I care about him.

OSVALDO: I love him.

FABIOLA

SONIA: Of course. He's your brother.

OSVALDO: And I hate him.

SONIA: No. Jealousy.

OSVALDO: Why should I be jealous of him?

SONIA: Oedipus.

OSVALDO: I don't know why you keep reading those books!

SONIA: They fascinate me. In the rest of the world everybody sees
psychiatrists. I only get to read about them.

Enter Pedro. He is carrying a rosary.

PEDRO: What a bunch of crap!

SONIA: It's religion.

PEDRO: Exactly.

SONIA: Religion is not crap.

PEDRO: No, worse than crap. (*He starts to twirl rosary*)

SONIA: Don't do that! It will turn into a snake and strangle you. (*She takes
the rosary*)

PEDRO: Who told you that?

SONIA: At catechism...

PEDRO: The nuns... (*He laughs*)

SONIA: Don't you dare laugh at the nuns.

OSVALDO: The priest told us the same thing.

PEDRO: Because they are all liars.

SONIA: No, don't be a blasphemer. It's not God's fault.

PEDRO: Yes it is, Sonia. It is precisely God's fault.

SONIA: How could it be?

PEDRO: If God plans everything, he planned this too. He planned what
has happened in my life.

OSVALDO: It adds up.

SONIA: What adds up?!

OSVALDO: What he said; it's logical.

SONIA: Except that all this could be the devil...the devil's work. Hmmm?

PEDRO: You don't really believe any of that, do you, Sonia?

SONIA: I want to. I want to believe it.

PEDRO: Why, Sonia?

OSVALDO: Because it makes life easier. Right, Sonia? It gives life a scheme.

SONIA: No. Because it makes life bearable. Heaven makes life bearable, and
I want life to be bearable, that's all.

PEDRO: You mean neat.

SONIA: Yes, I like to know where everything is.

PEDRO: You mean like my wife's body?

SONIA: And her spirit.

OSVALDO: She just saw her.

SONIA: No!

OSVALDO: You said you saw her!?

SONIA: I felt her.

PEDRO: She touched you?

SONIA: Yes, it was more like a caress over my entire body. It was soothing.

PEDRO: Soothing?

Pedro collapses on the floor. Pause.

OSVALDO: He's out.

SONIA: Too much booze. What shall we do? Wait till he comes to?

Pause.

OSVALDO: Get somebody to help prop him up.

SONIA: Sara. I think Sara is the best choice. Well, don't you think?

OSVALDO: Anybody but Mama, and Clara. Is he bleeding?

SONIA: Yes, his forehead.

OSVALDO: Get something to clean it with.

SONIA: Yes.

OSVALDO: Do you think one day he'll just drop dead?

SONIA: Don't say that. Don't even say that. Do *you* think he will?

Pause.

OSVALDO: Yes. Have you checked Oscar?

SONIA: Yes, before we started the rosary; no earache tonight, he's sleeping.

OSVALDO: Thank God. Tomorrow we're going to leave him at your mother's, right?

SONIA: Yes. Let me go and get help. He might have a concussion. (*She exits*)

OSVALDO: If you were only that lucky. They give operations now to make people forget. If I could tap the little part of my brain where you dwell, I would eliminate it from my head, Pedro.

PEDRO: God. . .

OSVALDO: But what would I be with that part of me gone? Hmmm? You stupid drunk. So you saw God?

FABIOLA

Pedro wakes up.

The first word that came out of your mouth was God. You fell down.
Don't get up, you fainted. Sonia is going for help.

PEDRO: You. You are my help.

OSVALDO: No, I'm your brother.

PEDRO: I don't care, do you? After the first time, it's not a matter of familial
ties. It becomes an ordinary thing.

OSVALDO: Yes.

PEDRO: Like going to a whore.

OSVALDO: Yes.

PEDRO: But safer.

OSVALDO: Yes. I don't know you. I don't know you a bit. Not a tiny little
bit of anything.

PEDRO: You know me like the lifeline in your hand.

Enter Sonia and Sara.

SONIA: Oh, you're awake.

OSVALDO: He just came to.

SONIA: Can't he talk?

PEDRO: Of course I can talk.

OSVALDO: Let's get him up.

Sara, Sonia and Osvaldo lift Pedro into a chair.

PEDRO: Slowly, my head is turning again.

OSVALDO: Oh shit, my back is hurting, shit!

Enter Clara.

PEDRO: I got what I need. (*He takes out a silver flask*) This is all I need.

CLARA: I knew there was something going on.

SONIA: What's he drinking?

Sara smells the flask.

SARA: Whiskey.

CLARA: The old J&B. He's full of blood! We can't let Cusa see him like this.

SONIA: Then be quiet, Clara. Osvaldo, walk him to the outside sink and
clean his face.

OSVALDO: All right.

SARA: Should I help?

OSVALDO: No, we can do it.

Exit Osvaldo and Pedro.

CLARA (*To Sara*): You'd like being outside in the dark with the men? (*To Sonia*) He's a wreck; you know that. We better start doing rosaries for him.

SONIA: I think he should go to a psychiatrist. I heard about a good one in El Vedado. I think he should go.

CLARA: Are you crazy?

SONIA: He could be helped. He's typical.

CLARA: Lazy is what he is.

SONIA: And what are you?

CLARA: A woman. I do what a woman is supposed to do; men are supposed to work.

SONIA: You're a lazy woman; you don't even try to improve your mind.

CLARA: My mind is fine. You think everyone should go to a psychiatrist.

SONIA: Maybe we all need it.

CLARA: You keep your opinions of this family to yourself. Just because you don't need them. Just because your father gives you an allowance. You're so spoiled, you have nothing to do but judge.

SONIA: You are the judge here, darling, not I. (*She starts to exit*) Sara, watch Oscar for me. If he cries, call me at my mother's, or take him to my mother's. I know it's late at night. But I can't stand this house at night. You'll be up till when?

SARA: Well, it's midnight now. Another hour. Do you need anything else?

SONIA: No, thank you. I'll come back here at one. Goodnight. (*She exits*)

CLARA: I'm not going to apologize to you for spitting at you.

SARA: Yes.

CLARA: I know I was right.

SARA: Yes.

CLARA: Someday, you'll be grateful to me for showing you what your place is.

SARA: You mean the way you must be grateful to Sonia.

CLARA: Why should I be grateful to Sonia? I'm not grateful to Sonia.

SARA: She shows you who you really are. (*She starts to exit*)

CLARA: Where are you going?

SARA: To get a towel for Pedro.

CLARA: I want café and milk.

SARA: The towel first.

CLARA: No, my café first.

SARA: No, the towel first. That's my duty, my obligation.

CLARA: No.

SARA: Yes. Pedro's mother and father pay for me. You're just the daughter-in-law. The son comes first; that's how I was trained. You see, I know my place.

CLARA: Tomorrow I have dresses for you to iron. I want my bedroom floor scrubbed.

Exit Sara.

And my husband's wardrobe rearranged! He's a son too! (*Pause*) Oh, Jesus, I'm alone. I don't like being in any room of this house alone. I scare me. Oh God, don't come to me, Fabiola. I don't want to see you. Just in my memory, cousin.

A record starts to play automatically.

Fabiola! OOOOOH! (*She runs from the room*)

Enter Miriam and Raulito.

MIRIAM: It's on the blink. It did that before she died, no big deal.

RAULITO: Sure?

MIRIAM: Yes, they do that. It's quirky. It was still on, so automatically the next record came down ten minutes later. But, electricity, not the beyond. (*She laughs*) What people don't want to admit, the reason why they believe in ghosts, I think, is out of ego. They can't believe that they'll never exist, that something has really changed, that something is gone, lost.

RAULITO: You're so smart.

MIRIAM: I'll sneak out later and meet you.

RAULITO: No.

MIRIAM: Coward.

RAULITO: I respect you.

MIRIAM: Why?

RAULITO: Because I want you someday to be my wife.

MIRIAM: So you deny me what I want; you're so stupid.

RAULITO: I'm proper.

MIRIAM: A fool is what you are.

RAULITO: I'm a good Catholic.

MIRIAM: Idiot. Do you know where my father is tonight? Whoring!

RAULITO: Well, he's a man.

MIRIAM: Then what are you?

RAULITO: I want to be your husband, and I want to be able to respect you.

MIRIAM: A bore, that's what you are, a self-righteous, spoiled little bore.

RAULITO: Stop it!

They exit. Enter Sonia, followed by Octavio and Pedro.

SONIA: We held a seance. Well, we tried to reach her spirit...

OCTAVIO: We found her. They made a mistake and they put her in the wrong mausoleum.

SONIA: Whose?

OCTAVIO: The Marquez's.

Exit Pedro.

SONIA: I'll get the others; they're doing a rosary.

Exit Sonia. Octavio looks around the dance floor. He goes to the piano and tries to touch one of the keys. We notice that he is wearing gloves. He screams in pain.

OCTAVIO: Bastards. Some day...

Enter Pedro.

PEDRO: Thank you, Octavio. So, she's safe. So it was all a mistake. You found her. It was such a strange thing. But she's safe; it's over.

The others enter.

CUSA: It's all settled?

OCTAVIO: Yes.

CONCHITA: Did you open the coffin to make sure it was her?

OCTAVIO: Yes.

CLARA: Did someone steal her jewelry?

OCTAVIO: No, cousin Clara.

PEDRO: Did she look...?

OCTAVIO: Beautiful...

Pause.

FABIOLA

SONIA: Asleep?

PEDRO: There must have been some decay.

OCTAVIO: No, it must be the marble. You have a marble mausoleum, no moisture gets into it, no worms. She looked perfect: beautiful, perfect and intact.

Pause.

CUSA: Like she was dreaming?

OCTAVIO: Yes, and happy at last.

OSVALDO: But intact. They used to make people saints who stayed intact.

MIRIAM: Or they called them vampires; depends on how much money you gave the priest.

SONIA: Why are you wearing gloves? They don't look right. They go with a tuxedo, not a shirt.

OCTAVIO: Batista.

SONIA: Batista?

OCTAVIO: They came after me; I didn't want to upset you.

SONIA: They questioned you.

CUSA: About who?

OCTAVIO: A revolutionary.

SONIA: Fidel Castro. My father told me about him.

CUSA: Are your hands hurting?

OCTAVIO: Yes. They stuck hot pins under my fingernails, and I know nothing about him, but they think I'm helping him. Three of my fingernails came off. They asked questions, but I had nothing to tell.

PEDRO: Intact? Intact! Intact! Intact!

Pause.

SONIA: I'll bandage them for you.

OCTAVIO: I don't want you to see that kind of ugliness.

CUSA: He's right; all the women leave the room.

RAULITO: I'm going home.

MIRIAM: We should all see it.

CLARA: It's nearly 1:00 A.M. (*She yawns*) Goodnight, sweet dreams.

Exit Clara and Raulito.

CUSA (*To Conchita*): Get bandages. (*To Miriam and Sonia*) You two go to bed.

MIRIAM: No.

CUSA: Yes.

OCTAVIO: For my sake.

SONIA: Let's go, Miriam.

Exit Miriam and Sonia. Pause.

OSVALDO: I'm going outside for a smoke. (*He exits*)

OCTAVIO: Please go.

CUSA: All right.

Exit Cusa with Conchita and Sara.

OCTAVIO: I want you to see it. (*He undoes his gloves; his hands are bloodied and burned*)

PEDRO: I can't help you.

Enter Alfredo.

ALFREDO: What's everybody doing up so late at night?

PEDRO: Praying. Help him.

ALFREDO: Look at them, Pedro.

PEDRO: I don't want to.

ALFREDO: Too ugly? What kind of man are you?

PEDRO: You'll help him. You're good at things like that. (*He exits*)

ALFREDO: Scared.

OCTAVIO: Spoiled.

ALFREDO: Spoiled rotten. But not as rotten as Batista. They caught up with you?

OCTAVIO: I didn't say a word. I had already given them the money.

ALFREDO: Good.

OCTAVIO: Tonight we bought Fidel three machine guns; it only cost me three fingernails.

ALFREDO: The maids will bandage your hands.

They exit. Enter Osvaldo and Pedro.

PEDRO: I'll do something crazy if you don't.

OSVALDO: No, you wouldn't.

PEDRO: Yes.

OSVALDO: Why?

PEDRO: Because I don't care. Let everybody know I was a bad husband. I was a pervert.

OSVALDO: That's not civilized.

FABIOLA

PEDRO: But it's what you want.

OSVALDO: She's still intact; that's a sign from God.

PEDRO: You're beginning to sound like your wife. (*Pause*) She knew.

OSVALDO: Fabiola?

PEDRO: Yes.

OSVALDO: About us? You told her?

PEDRO: She thought it was erotic.

OSVALDO: She did? Then that's why she's in purgatory. You see, no matter how you look at it, it's a sign.

PEDRO: She's not a saint.

OSVALDO: How much do you want?

PEDRO: The night. If you don't I'll drive down to Havana. I'll get myself arrested and they'll take out all my—

Enter Sonia.

SONIA: Osvaldo, I'm tired.

OSVALDO: I thought you were already in bed!

SONIA: I was waiting for you. So how awful was it?

OSVALDO: What!

PEDRO: His hands were a mess.

SONIA: He must be in terrible pain.

PEDRO: Oh, I think he felt heroic.

SONIA: Oh, let's go to bed, Osvaldo.

PEDRO: No. Osvaldo and I are going to the cemetery to take a look. Pain or no pain. I don't believe him. Want to come?

SONIA: No, don't go. Please, Osvaldo, wait. Don't go at night.

PEDRO: If I'm cursed, I want to see the evidence.

SONIA: See, you do believe in God.

OSVALDO: Go to bed. I have to go with him.

PEDRO: That's what a brother, a family is for.

SONIA: Goodnight. Be careful. Maybe you should tell your mother.

PEDRO: No.

Sonia starts to exit.

OSVALDO: Kiss me.

Sonia and Osvaldo kiss politely. Exit Sonia.

PEDRO: You want to?

OSVALDO: If you want it.

PEDRO: I do.

Pedro and Osvaldo go to the upstairs room. Sonia reenters the ballroom. She goes to the piano and starts to play.

SONIA: I'm sorry you had to die, Fabiola. (*She prays*)

Enter Sara. She begins to clean up. Pedro and Osvaldo enter the upstairs room. Osvaldo sits on the bed. Pedro stands in front of him.

PEDRO: There's nothing important in life, only sensations.

OSVALDO: Sensations.

Sonia is praying.

SONIA: Fabiola, was it painful?

PEDRO: That's all, sensations.

Pedro and Osvaldo kiss.

Scene 2

In the kitchen Sonia and Clara are sitting at the counter wrapping grapes with white and pink tissue paper. Sara is washing grapes. In the upstairs room Pedro and Osvaldo are naked, asleep on the bed. We see Miriam close the door to the upstairs room. She runs downstairs.

OSVALDO: What was that?

PEDRO: The wind.

OSVALDO: No one? Are you sure?

PEDRO: Maybe it was Fabiola; maybe she wants to join in.

OSVALDO: How dare you talk that way about the dead!

Miriam enters the kitchen.

MIRIAM: Wrapping grapes every New Year's Eve. Eat a grape at midnight and you'll be lucky. Well, I'm living proof that it's a lie. One year I ate twelve grapes and that year I had the mumps, the measles, a cold for three months and Mama caught me kissing my pillow.

CLARA: It's a custom. We have to do it.

MIRIAM: Why? Why do we have to do anything?

SONIA: Because it's normal.

MIRIAM: It's superstition. This whole house is full of—

SONIA: It's fun to wrap grapes.

CLARA: Superstition is the truth.

MIRIAM: The truth. Little black balls wrapped around our necks. Saints with apples at their feet and glasses of water. Bodies that won't disappear. . .

SONIA: Miriam, please, it's New Year's Eve. We are supposed to be happy.

MIRIAM: All these offerings. (*She takes the offering, an apple*) So Saint Barbara will do what Mama commands. Relics, icons; it's the Dark Ages. (*She bites into the apple*)

SONIA: Miriam, please stop.

CLARA: Oh my God.

Sonia takes the apple from her.

SARA: Jesus, forgive her. (*She crosses herself*)

MIRIAM: Saint Barbara is not going to give Mama her wish. She was just a spoiled princess who five hundred years ago pretended to be a soldier, and some guy cut off her head. And her father felt so ashamed when the town found out that his daughter was fooling around with soldiers that he paid a pope to make her a saint. And they all pretended that she was. And now Mama prays to her. Hmmm. What a joke.

CLARA: Don't you talk that way about Saint Barbara. She's performed many proven miracles for a lot of Cubans.

MIRIAM: I know, Clara, and every month last year was a good one because of a grape.

SONIA: I'm eating them no matter what you say. The new year has to be better.

CLARA: This one was no fun, having the house messed up three times in one month.

SONIA: Octavio told me he saw Osvaldo's name on Batista's list.

MIRIAM: They think he's part of the underground? A revolutionary? (*She laughs*)

SONIA: I think we should move in with my parents. They don't believe in politics and Batista's boys never bother them.

MIRIAM: We should all move.

CLARA: It would upset Cusa if we did.

MIRIAM: I'm going to let Raulito marry me. He asked me again this morning.

SONIA: Oh Miriam, that's the best news for the new year.

CLARA: I knew it.

MIRIAM: And I'm going to get my own house.

SONIA: I saw the most beautiful dress in the Paris *Vogue*. It had a Peter Pan collar and a bouffant skirt, perfect for you.

CLARA: I think you should wear a hat instead of a veil; it's more chic.

SONIA: Get married in April so it isn't too hot.

CLARA: Another big party. Sara, clean more grapes. It's going to cost Alfredo a bundle.

SONIA: I'll be a bridesmaid.

CLARA: Me too?

MIRIAM: I might not want a fancy wedding.

CLARA: Don't talk crazy.

Pause. The radio plays a fast version of "Guantanamera." The women continue to wrap grapes. Sara sets washed grapes in front of them.

MIRIAM: I think Fidel is sexy.

SONIA: Sexier than Batista.

MIRIAM: I bet you he smells of sweat.

CLARA: I bet he smells. Sara, are you sure you washed these grapes?

MIRIAM: And he's willing to fight.

SARA: Aren't they clean?

CLARA: No. Here, do them again. And we only need a few more.

SONIA: Sara, the grapes are fine. Leave her alone, Clara.

SARA: Sonia, I think Fidel should take a shower and shave.

Sonia and Sara laugh.

SONIA: He doesn't have time. He's a revolutionary. He's up in the hills fighting.

SARA: But what for?

SONIA: To get into power, to become our prime minister. After he overthrows Batista by force, revolution; he's going to have elections and he'll run for prime minister; and then he's going to stop prostitution.

MIRIAM: I think Fidel's a real man.

SONIA: Miriam!

MIRIAM: We need a real man.

CLARA: We've got plenty of real men around here.

MIRIAM: Really?

CLARA: My husband, he's a real man; Ricardo works.

MIRIAM: Daddy pays his salary, Clara.

CLARA: Still, he tells me he has to go to Havana every day at nine and keep records.

SONIA: Records of what?

CLARA: Alfredo's money. That's better than some.

SONIA: My husband has a university degree.

MIRIAM: Yes, he's very proper.

SONIA: Miriam! We'll monogram all your towels: big Rs and Ms intertwining.

CLARA: Going to a university is not work.

MIRIAM: I'm not good at embroidering.

SONIA: I'll teach you. It's a very relaxing thing to do while you wait, while you're waiting to get married.

MIRIAM: Sonia, maybe this family is too wicked for him.

SONIA: Don't worry, when he marries you he'll be firm and keep you in line.

Sonia and Miriam laugh.

CLARA: The only thing this family is is lazy. Except for my husband and Alfredo. Where's Raulito going to work?

MIRIAM: He's going to study.

CLARA: What?

MIRIAM: Something.

CLARA: Thank God for giving me a husband that works.

SONIA: Sara, do you like embroidering?

SARA: I like watching you embroider, you're so delicate.

SONIA: You are too.

SARA: I don't have time.

CLARA: Sara and Ricardo know what it's like to work for a living.

MIRIAM: Lucky them.

SONIA: Sara, what's it like?

SARA: You just wake up and do it.

Enter Cusa.

SONIA: Cusa, Miriam has great news. (*Pause*) Miriam, tell your mother.

MIRIAM: Not now.

CLARA: She thinks Raulito is going to ask for her hand.

CUSA: Are all the grapes wrapped? Twelve in each? It would be embarrassing if someone got eleven.

MIRIAM: So what! They would have one lousy month. What a stupid custom.

SONIA (*To Cusa*): You think Raulito's not good enough?

CUSA: You girls should get dressed. People are already arriving.

MIRIAM: Mama, you know the party has already started in the roof room. Osvaldo and Pedro have been up there drinking all day!!

SONIA: It's New Year's.

MIRIAM: It's always New Year's for them. (*Pause*) The happy drunks.

CUSA: Don't talk that way about your brothers. Go get dressed.

MIRIAM: I'm going to be a slut tonight.

CUSA: Sara pressed your dresses.

SONIA: Sara, you worked so hard today setting up the house and you remembered about our dresses. Thank you. (*She exits*)

SARA: I'm glad to do it.

Exit Miriam.

CLARA: Oh, you're so considerate. Happy New Year. Bring mine to my room.

Exit Clara. Sara follows. Cusa closes doors and turns on the radio. Fidel's voice is heard giving a speech promising victory. Cusa is totally caught up in the speech.

CUSA: Fidel! You will make us Cubans. You will free us!

The static picks up. She turns down the volume.

I'm going to light three candles and make an offering to the saint and when the new year comes, you will be in Havana—safe, victorious!

She lights three candles and places them at the base of the statue. Then she puts a glass of water and an apple next to the candles. After a moment's thought, she goes to the stove and dishes out a small bowl of paella which she places with the other offerings. Then she prays quietly, her prayer punctuated by three outbursts.

For Fidel!

She dips her fingers in the water and with a snap of her wrist, flicks water on the altar.

For Cuba!

She repeats the gesture.

For dignity!

She repeats the gesture and prays. Enter Alfredo, smoking a cigar. She looks him over.

When the new regime arrives you can go and live with the actress.

ALFREDO: It's the actress's sister. She's not an actress.

CUSA: You can live with both.

ALFREDO: Fine.

CUSA: The party has started. Go be debonair, Alfredo.

ALFREDO: Are you coming?

CUSA: No. Tonight will be me and the radio. Go.

ALFREDO: Have you eaten today?

CUSA: No. I won't eat till Fidel marches on Havana. Then I'll have a potato with a spoonful of olive oil on top. For now, milk and coffee; that's all.

ALFREDO: A true martyr.

Cusa switches the station. She hears something on the radio.

CUSA: See, listen, they just said it. They think tonight.

Alfredo listens.

ALFREDO: That's propaganda, to give people hope. Can't you tell the difference between propaganda and the real news, the truth?

Cusa listens to the radio.

CUSA: They're already in the province of Havana.

ALFREDO: That's what they say. I got it from the horse's mouth, and he assured—

CUSA: Who?!

ALFREDO: Aquiles.

CUSA: One of Batista's generals; what do you expect him to say?

ALFREDO: That shows how much you know; sometimes you act retarded. Aquiles has direct contact with Fidel. He's one of Fidel's closest men; he saved Fidel's life. He's going to be our contact with the new government. He has direct contact with Fidel Castro, so if he says a week, it's a week. So no more silly talk, don't tell me rumors. I have indirectly-direct contact with Fidel.

CUSA: The Voice of America is the voice of the people. I believe them, not some cheap politician. And I know he'll be in Havana tonight.

ALFREDO: Let's just hope he gets here. Relax, it'll happen. (*He exits*)

CUSA (*To Saint Barbara*): Shoot loud, Fidel. Hear it, America.

As the door opens we can hear a rock-and-roll tune being played by the band in the ballroom. There's laughter inside. Enter Raulito. He carries a bottle of champagne and two glasses.

RAULITO: Cusa . . .

CUSA: Raulito. (*Pause*) How are you?

RAULITO (*Smiling earnestly*): In heaven.

Pause.

CUSA (*Without enthusiasm*): Yes?

RAULITO: I talked to Alfredo. He said. (*Pause*) Yes. Miriam and I are going to announce our engagement tonight. (*Pause*) We want you to be there.

Pause. Cusa turns away from Raulito and puts her ear to the radio.

I love her very much. I'll be good to her, I promise.

Cusa doesn't respond.

I *love* her.

Cusa doesn't respond.

I respect her.

Cusa turns to him.

CUSA: She's not good for you.

RAULITO: How could you say that?

CUSA: Forget her.

RAULITO: I could never forget her! I adore her!

Cusa lets her attention go to the radio for a moment, then she studies Raulito.

CUSA: She's been to bed with others. You know that?

RAULITO: I love Miriam. I think you're exaggerating things.

CUSA: You'll end up like me. She's just like Alfredo.

Raulito very deliberately pours a glass of champagne. He drinks it. Then he fills the other glass and sets it in front of Cusa.

RAULITO: You will come for the toast.

CUSA: I'll toast when Fidel is in Havana.

Raulito goes to the door.

RAULITO: We are waiting till midnight. (*Pause*) We will be very happy.

Cusa doesn't respond.

Happy New Year.

Exit Raulito. Cusa puts her ear back to the radio. Enter Conchita carrying a box filled with fruits.

CONCHITA (*Singing*):
Wake up my darling, wake up.
The sun has come out to look.
All the little birds are singing;
The moon has gone for a rest.

That's what my husband sang every Saturday morning by my bedroom window.

CUSA: So did my husband, God save his soul. (*She crosses herself*)

CONCHITA: They all did. It was the style then. (*Pause*) Here is the last box of fruit from the farm; they brought mangoes, bananas, coconuts, malangas, avocados...

CUSA: Put them in the outside sink.

CONCHITA: The little boy said: "Many thanks to Señora Cusa for letting my family work her farm for yet another year; this makes twenty happy years together."

Enter Miriam in a party dress.

MIRIAM: Three minutes!! (*She exits*)

CUSA: Such a handsome boy.

CONCHITA: "Say to her Happy New Year for her and her family. May 1959 bring the best."

CUSA: How nice of him. Maybe it will.

CONCHITA: We should make an offering to the saint.

CUSA: I already did.

Enter Sonia in a party dress.

SONIA: Two minutes!

The radio begins playing "Begin The Beguine." Exit Sonia. Lights up on the upstairs room. Music from the ballroom drifts up through the floor. Pedro and Osvaldo are drinking from a silver flask.

PEDRO (*Whispering*): What a way to end the year.

OSVALDO: What do you mean?

PEDRO: With your cock in my mouth.

OSVALDO: Don't be filthy. Don't think about it. Don't say it. I don't like you to say it that way. I don't like you to name it.

PEDRO: I won't utter a sound. Whatever you want. Always whatever you want.

OSVALDO: I should go greet the new year with Sonia. She expects that.

Sound of gunshots.

Fighting on New Year's! Hah!

PEDRO: Fidel or Batista?

CUSA (*In the kitchen*): Open all the windows so we can hear the gunshots!

PEDRO: They took so long. They had her wait in the delivery room for three days, and all I thought about was how much I loved you.

Osvaldo kisses Pedro's hand, then he begins to dress.

The baby was born a boy. I had a boy. It was too big, the baby; he killed her.

OSVALDO: Fidel was a wild guy. He once drove his MG into a wall at the university.

PEDRO: She didn't want to die.

OSVALDO: That's why she remains intact. (*Pause*) Tonight was the end!

PEDRO: She wanted to breast-feed the baby, the little boy, but it had already been buried.

OSVALDO: No more sex. I can't have any more sex with you.

Pedro drinks from the flask. Octavio enters the kitchen.

OCTAVIO: Cuba is free! We won! We beat the bastards! Alfredo!

Exit Octavio. Exit Conchita. Applause is heard amidst shouts of "Happy New Year" and "Cuba Libre." Cusa crosses to the stove and begins to eat from the paella pot. Enter Alfredo. He is smoking a cigar.

CUSA: The liberator is here.

ALFREDO: Batista left in a private plane. Fidel will be in Havana tomorrow.

CUSA: Now we will be free.

ALFREDO: Now you can eat something.

They kiss. Exit Alfredo. Cusa eats.

PEDRO (*Upstairs*): She had a child. That's what we were supposed to do. Isn't that right?

Sonia enters the kitchen. She is carrying a paper package.

SONIA: I have twelve grapes for Osvaldo. He said he'd be down at midnight, but Pedro must be depressed. Osvaldo has become Pedro's psychiatrist.

CUSA: This paella is delicious.

SONIA: Maybe now that it's all beginning, Pedro won't be so sad. Maybe the demons will leave him alone. Maybe now. . .

CUSA: She's still intact. Four years and she's still intact. You should get twelve grapes for Pedro too.

SONIA: I'm sorry, you're right, but it's past midnight. It won't work anyway.

CUSA: We won't need grapes this year. You should have another baby, Sonia. The world is worth being in now. Did Miriam and Raulito announce their engagement yet?

SONIA: No, with all the excitement. . .

CUSA: Well, I'll announce it for them. (*She takes the glass of champagne*)

SONIA: Good. You changed your mind.

Enter Osvaldo.

CUSA: Yes, it's time to give everything a chance. We've had a revolution. Happy New Year, Sonia. Happy New Year, Osvaldo. (*She exits*)

SONIA: You're late.

OSVALDO: I'm sorry.

SONIA: Eat the grapes anyway. You have to finish all twelve in one minute.

Pause. Osvaldo eats.

Batista's gone; Fidel is here! It's so nice to see your mother enjoying a meal, celebrating. . . . There's talk that the whole city of Havana is going out into the street tomorrow morning with flags and signs saying Welcome Home Fidel! Can we go?

OSVALDO: It might be dangerous.

Pause.

SONIA: Osvaldo, you know how I want to celebrate? I want Oscar to have a little sister.

OSVALDO: Another brat. Are you drunk!

SONIA: I'm not the one who gets drunk! (*Pause*) Fidel is going to make everybody happy.

OSVALDO: He will?

SONIA: Yes. (*She kisses him passionately*) If it's a boy we will name him Fidel.

PEDRO (*Upstairs*): Fabiola, the child was born dead. (*He starts to cry*)

END OF ACT ONE

FABIOLA

ACT TWO

Scene 1

The kitchen. Alfredo and Cusa are in the middle of a fight. Cusa has just turned off the radio.

ALFREDO: Kennedy's Catholic; he won't let us down. He's a good boy!

CUSA: You thought Fidel was a good boy too.

ALFREDO: I never did.

CUSA: He fooled you. So will Kennedy.

ALFREDO: We needed to give Batista a good kick in the ass. Fidel was convenient, that's all. The one in love was you!

CUSA: Yes, and he betrayed me!

ALFREDO: Calm down. It's only politics, not life.

Pause. The sound of gunshots is heard.

I think we should all go hide at the farm.

CUSA: I'm staying in my house; the farm no longer belongs to us. Tomorrow Osvaldo will hand them the papers and it will be theirs, the USSR's.

ALFREDO: It will be the Nation's, darling.

CUSA: I hope Russians like bananas.

ALFREDO: It's not my fault.

CUSA: But you've always had it under control, Alfredo.

ALFREDO: Don't start.

CUSA: You'd come home, pockets full of money to impress the children, to buy them with stolen money.

ALFREDO: That was almost thirty years ago.

CUSA: Twenty-three. One night you threw thirty thousand dollars in cash all over our bed while I was sleeping.

ALFREDO: I was just showing off.

CUSA: You woke me up. I told you I wasn't for sale, that I was different than your whores, that you didn't impress me.

ALFREDO: That's why I stopped coming home! That's why!

CUSA: I don't care. The Americans colonized us with dollars. People like you let them do it.

ALFREDO: That's why I had to run out of my own house.

THE FLOATING ISLAND PLAYS

CUSA: Now Castro is letting the Russians in. We have to stop him. I want my country back.

Enter Octavio, running.

OCTAVIO: Where's Osvaldo?

CUSA: At the farm.

OCTAVIO: There's a list. Two milicianos came to my father's house. They told him they wanted him, my brother and me. He tried to punch him; they shot him in the leg, maybe somewhere else; I don't know. In the struggle they dropped their list. My mother picked it up for them; she saw my name, my brother's name, my father's name and Osvaldo's name. I left and ran here to tell you. There's a list, they know, and Osvaldo's on it.

CUSA: Why not me?

OCTAVIO: There's no women on it. From your house only Osvaldo.

ALFREDO: We'll sneak both of you out through the embassy. We'll plan something that'll work.

CUSA: Something better than the last time.

OCTAVIO: We thought that was a good plan.

CUSA: And your poor godfather got shot and died. I told you it wouldn't work; you two would not listen. To pretend to be a fruit vendor in front of the Swiss Embassy and then run for it!

ALFREDO: I'll plan a better escape for my son. We'll do it at night.

CUSA: Learn from your mistakes.

ALFREDO: Octavio, go to the farm. Use my car. Tell Osvaldo to come home.

CUSA: Don't tell him why.

OCTAVIO: He should know!

CUSA: He would panic. So would Sonia. Tell her to stay at the farm.

OCTAVIO: They have no idea about what's going on?

CUSA: No.

ALFREDO: After you tell him, you go hide in my office...the back room. I'll knock three times in the morning and sing "Diamonds Are a Girl's Best Friend" when the coast is clear, and we can sneak you over to the—

OCTAVIO: No. After I tell him, I'm taking a boat, a raft, or swimming out of this place to some sort of freedom. Even if I don't speak the language!

CUSA: A lot of people die.

OCTAVIO: I'd rather be eaten by sharks than by them, than by Fidel.

CUSA: Here comes Miriam. Go.

Enter Miriam.

MIRIAM: You look like you've seen a ghost.

OCTAVIO: No, it's just real life. (*He exits*)

MIRIAM: Well? Why's the radio not on? We are losing, aren't we?

Enter Conchita and Raulito.

They know we are a part of it?

ALFREDO: Never mind.

CUSA: Yes, Miriam, they do.

ALFREDO: We'll win!

CONCHITA: Let's pray.

MIRIAM: No. Let's listen to the radio.

Miriam turns on the radio. Static is heard. Upstairs Pedro does a rosary. Cusa lights a candle to Saint Barbara.

PEDRO: Hail Mary full of. . .no, it doesn't work. Fabiola, full of. . .that doesn't work either. (*He lights a cigarette and turns off the lamp*)

In the kitchen a miliciano appears. Miriam, seeing him, changes the station on the radio.

MILICIANO 1: No big news; it's just a little shooting.

ALFREDO: What do you want?

MILICIANO 1: Osvaldo Marquez. (*He points to Raulito*) Are you him?

MIRIAM: No, he's my husband. You know that.

RAULITO: Raul.

MIRIAM: Not anything like a Marquez.

MILICIANO 1: Who's Osvaldo Marquez?

ALFREDO: My son.

CONCHITA: You knock before you come in this house.

ALFREDO: Why are you looking for my son?

MILICIANO 1: His name's on my list.

ALFREDO: List?

MILICIANO 1: Conspirators to the Bay of Pigs.

ALFREDO: My son's vacationing.

MILICIANO 1: Where?

CUSA: In Varadero, on the beach.

MILICIANO 1: I have to search the house. (*Pause. He shouts outside*) Paco!

Enter Miliciano 2.

MILICIANO 2: Which way are the rooms?

ALFREDO: This way. (*He points to the hall door*)

Exit Milicianos 1 and 2.

CONCHITA: Pedro.

CUSA: Quiet.

Long pause. Milicianos 1 and 2 reenter. Miliciano 2 waits in the kitchen. Miliciano 1 goes to the upstairs room. Pedro is lying in bed. All the lights are off.

PEDRO: Osvaldo?

MILICIANO 1: Are you Osvaldo Marquez?

PEDRO: Why?

MILICIANO 1: You are Osvaldo Marquez?

PEDRO: Why not?

MILICIANO 1: Turn on the light.

PEDRO: No.

MILICIANO 1: No? I'm ordering you.

PEDRO: You have a gun?

MILICIANO 1: Yes.

PEDRO: Who are you? (*He turns on a light*) Oh, I remember you. You used to sell bait for fishing. You remember me. I caught that big swordfish. . .

MILICIANO 1: That was a long time ago.

PEDRO: Couple of years. You were impressed. How many pounds was it? You remember? It was a monster, wasn't it?

MILICIANO 1: Pedro Marquez.

PEDRO: You remember me.

MILICIANO 1: The oldest. The one with the red Jaguar. . .not on my list.

PEDRO: J&B?

MILICIANO 1: All right, a sip. Americans do make good whiskey.

PEDRO: What list?

MILICIANO 1: You know.

PEDRO: No. I stay up here now. I don't know anything now.

MILICIANO 1: Stop making a fool of me. Everybody knows they've invaded.

PEDRO: Who?

MILICIANO 1: Worms from your class. Greedy people like you. They don't make very good soldiers.

PEDRO: I imagine not.

FABIOLA

MILICIANO 1: They thought it would be easy. Can I have another sip?

PEDRO: You can have all you want. It belongs to you.

MILICIANO 1: Not to me, to the revolution. It's everybody's. (*He drinks*) They got conned. The Americans finally realized that we had surpassed them. Our belief was stronger than their power.

PEDRO: What does that have to do with Osvaldo? He didn't do anything. We don't believe in things like that.

MILICIANO 1: Sure, you're all greedy. You all want your Jaguars.

PEDRO: Do you want to have it?

MILICIANO 1: What?

PEDRO: The Jaguar—the red one—you can have it. Look in the closet: dozens of suits, silk shirts, Italian shoes. It belongs to you. Take this comb. . . real silver. I don't care. You can have it, yes?

MILICIANO 1: Not till we get rid of you. Not till your kind disappears. Where's your brother?

PEDRO: My wife? You can have her. Fabiola.

MILICIANO 1: She's dead.

PEDRO: But she hasn't disappeared, she looks the same. People say she walks around at night! You can have anything here! It's yours. But not Osvaldo.

MILICIANO 1: He's all I have to find. Where is he?

PEDRO: With his wife, second honeymoon. He's nothing; you don't want him.

MILICIANO 1: He's a criminal, a murderer. He tried to destroy the greatest revolution on the face of the earth.

PEDRO: By himself. (*He laughs*)

MILICIANO 1: Don't. He helped. You're not people, you're leeches.

PEDRO: Take me then. I'm Osvaldo. I'm just like him, greedy. We're all greedy.

MILICIANO 1: Your name's not on the list.

Exit Miliciano 1. Pedro watches him from the top of the staircase.

PEDRO: It would give me something to do. We have the same last name! Who would know?!

Miliciano 1 enters the kitchen.

MILICIANO 1: How well you live. Do any of you recall the name? The hotel?

MIRIAM: The Hilton, I think. Yes, the Varadero Hilton.

MILICIANO 1: Of course.

Exit Milicianos 1 and 2.

CONCHITA: We've got to get to the farm and tell Osvaldo.

RAULITO: I told you you should get a phone for the farm.

MIRIAM: They listen in on the phone, Raulito. I'll go; I'll volunteer.

CUSA: It's been taken care of.

MIRIAM: Octavio running our errands again.

RAULITO: What will they do if they catch him?

ALFREDO: Kill him.

RAULITO: Oh, it's serious; it's life and death! There's no one we can offer money to?

CUSA: Not anyone that would make a difference.

PEDRO (*Upstairs*): Osvaldo! They're going fishing!

RAULITO: If he keeps screaming they'll come back! Get him to shut up!

PEDRO: Osvaldo!!

ALFREDO: Raulito, be a man!

Cusa starts to exit.

RAULITO: Don't tell him anything! He'll lose control. He'd drive to the farm.

MIRIAM: Give him a drink. Get him to pass out.

Exit Cusa.

ALFREDO: Let's lock all the doors and windows.

Exit Alfredo, Miriam, Raulito and Conchita. Cusa enters the upstairs room.

CUSA: Pedro, it's too dangerous to sleep here tonight. Come downstairs.

PEDRO: When did they start making lists? I thought only Batista made lists.

CUSA: Just tonight, sleep in your room.

PEDRO: Where is Osvaldo? I need him!

CUSA: Pedro, you have to be strong.

PEDRO: They think Osvaldo's part of the underground. I thought the underground was above ground now!

CUSA: Fidel let us down . . .

PEDRO: I have to warn Osvaldo. Osvaldo! Run!

CUSA: Quiet! Osvaldo went down to the farm.

PEDRO: Why did Sonia go?

CUSA: To be with her husband. Pedro, when we die our country has to belong to us.

PEDRO: I don't give a shit about that. I need to relax.

Cusa pours him a drink.

CUSA: He has to go. Osvaldo has to go or they'll kill him.

Pedro starts to cry.

PEDRO: I'll be alone.

CUSA: It's hard to lose people. My mother died. Then my father died. I was only sixteen.

PEDRO: I don't cry for Fabiola.

CUSA: I kept going. You know what freedom means?

Pedro gulps his drink.

PEDRO: Whatever keeps you calm and lets you sleep. I want to remember nice times. Sing me to sleep.

CUSA: If things were democratic, our class wouldn't be blamed for all the ugly things! For the whims of corrupt men.

PEDRO: Men's whims. (*He pours himself a drink*) I want to remember nice times. The one about the little boat.

CUSA: You're too old for songs.

PEDRO (*Singing*): There was once a tiny little boat. There was once a tiny little boat. There was once a tiny little boat, that just couldn't, that just couldn't, that just couldn't sail away...

CUSA: I used to tell you stories about Cuba. Remember them, Pedro? How we were discovered by Christopher Columbus and he said: "This is the most beautiful land that human eyes have seen."

PEDRO (*Singing*): He tried for one two three four five six seven weeks. He tried for one two three four five six seven weeks. He tried for one two three four five six seven weeks...

CUSA: And how the Spaniards and the Africans came. And how people, after they'd been here together through a couple of generations, started calling themselves Cubans...

PEDRO (*Singing*): ... but the little boat just couldn't, just couldn't sail away. And if the story doesn't seem long enough. And if the story doesn't seem long enough...

CUSA: ... natives of a new land. So they fought to be Cubans, to have an identity. But how could you believe me? How could even a little boy believe in something that never really existed?

PEDRO (*Singing*): We will repeat it, we will repeat it, we will repeat it once again. There was once a tiny little boat...

CUSA: When you live through one dictator after another, after another, then one more. (*Pause*) When all you ever really wanted to do was pick up a gun and kill everyone that oppressed you. (*Pause*) I should have told you to do that when you were a little boy. Do it now, Pedro.

PEDRO: Mother, I can't move.

CUSA: Cubans are killing each other again, that's all. Pedro, no one can move.

Exit Cusa. Downstairs Miriam is listening to the radio.

MIRIAM: Surrendered!

RAULITO: The Voice of America said it?

MIRIAM: No, Radio Free Europe.

RAULITO: Behave!

Enter Alfredo.

MIRIAM: It's all lost.

Long pause. "The Internationale" is heard playing over loudspeakers from a truck outside.

ALFREDO: "Prisoners of starvation"? "Masses of the world"? We lost in less than three days.

Sound of gunfire. They fall to the floor. Enter Conchita.

CONCHITA: It's starting again?!

The following dialogue overlaps. Gunfire gets louder.

RAULITO: Wow, I think I'm getting the runs. Our Father who art in heaven.... Oh my God! Oh my God! I am sorry. I confess all my sins because of thy just punishment.

MIRIAM: Hail Mary, full of grace, because of my sins, because I'm not worthy.

CONCHITA: My guardian angel, sweet companion. Thy kingdom come; thy...

RAULITO: I believe in life after death, in...

MIRIAM: In one holy Catholic church.

ALFREDO: The...the...the...

CUSA: The forgiveness of sins.

FABIOLA

Sound of glass shattering.

ALL: In the name of the Father, the Son, the Holy...

RAULITO: My God! I am getting the runs! (*He exits, crawling*)

MIRIAM: You won't let it happen, will you? You're not going to let them kill Osvaldo, are you? You'll make sure we're all safe?

ALFREDO: I'll try.

Sound of "The Internationale" grows louder. Gunfire stops.

MIRIAM: Listen to it! Listen to how loud it is!

CUSA: You should go and see if Raulito is all right.

MIRIAM: He can wipe his own ass.

CONCHITA: Miriam!

MIRIAM: There's no reason to be proper anymore.

CUSA (*To Saint Barbara*): If they catch him.... I would have given you my son, Saint Barbara! I offered you my life!

MIRIAM: Offer her this house! Offer her this country! Saint Barbara, if we survive I promise to believe in the Catholic Church and I won't get a divorce.

Music grows louder.

The truck that's playing "The Internationale" will be playing in front of our house soon.

ALFREDO: We'll dance a rhumba when it plays.

MIRIAM: I prefer a cha cha cha. Protect me.

ALFREDO: Always. (*He sings*) Arise ye prisoners of starvation, cha cha cha...

MIRIAM: Arise ye wretched of the earth, cha cha cha...

RAULITO (*Offstage*): Help me! I want to puke! Ohhhh!

ALFREDO: I better go see if Raulito is...if I can calm him down. (*Pause*) We will win! (*He exits*)

CUSA: "For hunger thunders condemnation. A new world's at birth..."

MIRIAM: Real life. Octavio said this was real life. I think he's right.

CUSA: Who knows?

MIRIAM: I hope he's wrong.

Enter Osvaldo.

OSVALDO: Mama! What's going on? Octavio showed up; he walked right into my bedroom, told me I was involved, I have to run because they would find me!?

CUSA: Go now, Conchita.

CONCHITA: I would not say a word.

CUSA: I know that.

CONCHITA: I'm one of the working people. They don't mess with me. (*She exits*)

CUSA: Sonia stayed at the farm, yes?

OSVALDO: No, she took Oscar to her mother's; she wants him to sleep there.

CUSA: We surrendered. It didn't work. They're arresting anyone involved in any way. You have to hide. Then I'll get you into the Swiss Embassy.

OSVALDO: I'm not going anywhere. I don't want to.

CUSA: You have to. You're involved, Osvaldo. Are there any priests left at the university?

OSVALDO: Yes, a few.

CUSA: Then that's where you should go. Miriam, get your father.

Exit Miriam.

OSVALDO: Involved? How was I involved?

CUSA: You are involved because I am involved. You ran an errand for me, the day you took that big box to Octavio's house.

OSVALDO: The one filled with old shoes.

CUSA: Revolvers.

Enter Alfredo and Miriam.

OSVALDO: Do I have to go to another country? Can't I just hide for a while?

ALFREDO: Fidel makes traitors dig their own graves and then shoots them.

OSVALDO: And I'm a traitor?

CUSA: Alfredo, get dressed. Drive to her house; that's what you do every night. They won't suspect anything. Just a little later than usual. Drop him off on the way. Yes, Alfredo?

ALFREDO: Where?

CUSA: The university.

ALFREDO: I'll get ready. (*He exits*)

CUSA: I'll make café.

OSVALDO: Pedro?

CUSA: Asleep.

OSVALDO: Upstairs?

CUSA: Yes.

Exit Osvaldo.

FABIOLA

MIRIAM: The radio. The radio will be our salvation. (*She turns on the radio*)

CUSA: Do you have any idea where Conchita keeps the café?

MIRIAM: Why would I?

CUSA: I've seen her put it away, but where? Maybe this is what they meant. Maybe this is what being privileged is about: you don't know where anything is kept, even in a kitchen of the house where you spent your life. (*She crosses to cupboard*) Oh, it is there!

Cusa begins to make coffee. Miriam listens to the radio. Osvaldo enters the upstairs room.

OSVALDO: Pedro, why do you want to be in this room?

PEDRO: To be away from you. (*Pause*) This guy came looking for you. He woke me up. Apparently they want you. Stupid Osvaldo. So proper and so stupid.

OSVALDO: My name's on the Bay of Pigs list! And I don't know why! Fidel—

PEDRO: Other people suffer besides you! (*He drinks*)

OSVALDO: She didn't decompose so you've become a drunk. They're making them dig their own graves and shooting them.

PEDRO: Who?

OSVALDO: Conspirators.

PEDRO: Have a drink.

OSVALDO: No.

PEDRO: For me.

Osvaldo takes the drink.

OSVALDO: I adore you, my big brother.

They drink. In the kitchen Miriam is listening to the radio. Cusa is waiting for the coffee to boil. Enter Sonia.

SONIA: The Bay of Pigs!

MIRIAM: Who are the pigs: us or them?

Sonia slaps her.

SONIA: Shut up! After tonight we'll be apart like a divorced couple. On the way back from the farm we had to drive through Havana, and all the lights were out. The only people on the streets were milicianos. They had machine guns and grenades and they looked up every couple of minutes.

MIRIAM: Looking for planes.

SONIA: They all looked panicked.

CUSA: Scared?

SONIA: Yes.

CUSA: Good.

MIRIAM: It all happened so fast. I got Fidel's autograph, his picture autographed by him with a dedication to me. Aquiles got it for me.

CUSA: Aquiles has already gone to the USA.

MIRIAM: "For Miriam. Help me build a new world. With much love and hope, Fidel Castro." I bought a silver frame for it. I kept it by my bed.

SONIA: I remember, yes. It made you very popular.

MIRIAM: One day I found it on the floor torn up.

SONIA: At first we thought Clara did it. She denied it though. All she ever got was a picture of Che without a dedication.

MIRIAM (*To Cusa*): You tore up that picture!

CUSA: Fidel has people working for him that are worse than your father. Imagine a world where your father is decent. I tore up anything that reminded me of Fidel. Marti said: "The United States—"

MIRIAM: "—got rid of the Spaniards for us. But who will get rid of the United States?" Fidel did do that for you, Mama.

CUSA: But he replaced them with Russians who are barbarians, who go nude swimming. Who have worse manners than Americans.

MIRIAM: They are taller and blonder.

SONIA: Tonight Havana looked like a dead city.

PEDRO (*Upstairs*): I always thought she was the real beauty, more than anyone else.

OSVALDO: I did too. I loved her. If I close my eyes I can see her, Fabiola, her green eyes, white skin. I remember the way she played the piano.

PEDRO: Yes.

They kiss.

If I could escape for you, I would. Go. Get out! Tell them I'm asleep. (*He pretends to be asleep*)

OSVALDO: Your new game?

PEDRO: Smart, huh?

Osvaldo laughs. Exit Osvaldo.

CUSA (*In the kitchen*): But it will be over before Christmas.

SONIA: Yes? Good. Praise be to God.

Enter Osvaldo.

OSVALDO: He was out.

SONIA: Drunk.

OSVALDO: Yes, drunk. I left him a note.

SONIA: That's nice. He'll miss you. I'll miss you. The new baby will miss you.

MIRIAM: You're pregnant? Beat me to it.

SONIA: Again, yes.

CUSA: When the baby is born everything will be better than before.

OSVALDO: Yes. We'll be in the U.S. of A.

SONIA: Don't even think that!

OSVALDO: It was a joke.

MIRIAM: When I saw that picture torn I knew.

CUSA: Café.

They sit and drink coffee silently. Enter Alfredo. He touches Osvaldo's shoulder.

SONIA: Osvaldo!

OSVALDO: Let's not show a thing.

CUSA: Turn away your face.

Exit Alfredo and Osvaldo.

SONIA: The milicianos in Havana are drinking beer on the holy altar, taking gold from the altar itself, dancing in the churches, defying God.

CUSA: We are not going to let them get us!

Upstairs Pedro begins to write in lipstick on the mirrored closet.

SONIA: The rings from the widows so their husbands could leave purgatory, they took them off the Virgin Mary's fingers. And their wives, the milicianos' wives, girls that went to catechism, carrying bags filled with God's gold to help their husbands.

MIRIAM: They got us where they want us.

Sonia and Cusa drink the café.

PEDRO (*Reading from the mirror*): "Osvaldo left April 22, 1961."

Scene 2

The ballroom. A sunny afternoon. Enter Sonia and Miriam. They are carrying bunches of roses. The roses are different colors; some of them have already opened up.

MIRIAM: I'm leaving in a week. I won't be able to come back once I get on the plane. I won't be able to come back till Fidel is gone, and today is probably the last May Day that I'll be able to bring flowers to the Virgin Mary.

SONIA: You mother wants you to take Saint Barbara with you to the United States where she'll be safe.

MIRIAM: So Saint Barbara will be a refugee too. (*Pause*) Why did I have to get a visa to that place? Why couldn't I have gone to Jamaica or Spain? Why do I have to end up in the USA?

SONIA: They're always pleasant there.

MIRIAM: This time we're not staying at the Fontainebleau. We are staying in Hialeah, that ugly place that I drove past once. And I'll have to expect Americans to be nice to me. You know they treat dogs better than they treat people.

SONIA: That's not true. They've always been nice to us.

MIRIAM: When it's convenient for them. Can't you see that?

SONIA: No.

MIRIAM: We were just a diversion for them, but Fidel got rid of their diversions: their pineapple company, the samba, the rhumba. . . . So now we're drowning.

SONIA: It has to end soon. They have to overthrow Fidel. I can't go to Hialeah; I belong a block away from my mother and father's house.

MIRIAM: I'm scared, Sonia.

They hug.

SONIA: We all are. Isn't this rose pretty?

MIRIAM: I took everything for granted.

SONIA: It smells wonderful too.

MIRIAM: The money, the beach, this house. . .

Enter Clara, followed by Conchita, who is carrying scissors. Enter Sara carrying a box full of roses.

CLARA: When I was little, my whole family would stand on the street waiting for the procession. I held two flowers, one in each hand. The Virgin would pass by; I'd throw two flowers. Then I'd look up and see the important families sitting at their windows throwing hundreds of roses. I thought: why do they have so many? (*To Miriam*) The first day your brother brought me here, he said: "That's the rose garden," and he pointed to the right. I saw it, and I knew I was in love.

SONIA: No procession this year.

MIRIAM: Is Mama still cutting roses?

CLARA: We're lucky we get to bring them to the church.

CONCHITA: We heard loud noises at the Alonsos. She went to look.

SONIA (*Admiring the roses*): So many different colors; I love yellow ones the best.

CONCHITA: Well, it's time for the unpleasant task.

MIRIAM: Cutting the thorns.

CLARA: Why bother?

SONIA: So no one pricks themselves at church.

CLARA: I don't think we need to do that.

CONCHITA: Here are the scissors.

SONIA: Thank you.

CONCHITA: Clara.

CLARA: All right. Sara, hand me a bunch.

Sara grabs a bunch of roses from the box.

SARA: Ooh!

CONCHITA: What is it?

SARA: I stuck a thorn in my finger.

CONCHITA: See why we have to do this! Let me look at it. (*She takes Sara's hand*) Which one?

SARA: The little finger.

Conchita tries to remove the thorn.

CONCHITA: I can't do it.

SONIA: I have long nails. Let me try. It must hurt.

She takes Sara's hand. Clara watches.

I see it. (*She pulls*) Out! See, it didn't hurt. Miriam, get a Band-Aid.

MIRIAM: Sure. (*She exits*)

SONIA: Your hands are all cut up.

CLARA: They look awful. You should wear rubber gloves.

SARA: They don't do any good.

CLARA: How is a man going to fall in love with your hands? Haven't you heard of manicures?

SARA: They don't do any good.

SONIA: Clara, shut up.

CLARA: I have a right to ask. Have you ever had your nails done?

SARA: Yes, but then I come here and scrub your toilets, do your dishes, give your children baths, scrub the floors—sometimes with ice water; and the fingernail polish disappears. I have to come here because I have to eat.

Enter Miriam.

MIRIAM: Here's the stuff.

SONIA: Put out your finger.

SARA: No, thank you. I'll do it myself.

SONIA: All right. I'm sorry.

Enter Cusa.

CUSA: The Alonsos left last night.

SONIA: How do you know?

CUSA: Fidel's milicia is living there now. Searching her house, the pigs. Wearing her hats, imitating her.

MIRIAM: Is that what they'll do when we go?

CUSA: Yes.

SONIA: Let's go look through the windows. We can see what they're doing through the windows.

Miriam, Sonia and Clara exit through the hall doors. Pause.

SARA: They used to stand in front of their windows and call us names.

CUSA: Who?

SARA: Mrs. Alonso's sons. They made fun of us.

CONCHITA: They were kidding with us.

SARA: They were mean and cruel.

Enter Sonia.

FABIOLA

SONIA: They're throwing photos out onto the street, and all her letters.

Enter Miriam.

MIRIAM: They have to be stopped. People's lives can't be dumped into a street.

Enter Clara, hysterical.

CLARA: They're throwing her underwear out, and her bras all over the street...hanging from the trees. Some are in our yard.

MIRIAM: We're going out to the street, and we'll pick everything up.

CONCHITA: Just stay in the house. If you don't look, you won't know what they're doing.

MIRIAM: If my life was on the street, I would want someone to protect it. Let's go pick up her things.

CLARA: I'm scared.

MIRIAM: We have to pick up her things.

CLARA: You're right, fuck them! Excuse the language.

CUSA: They'll yell at us. Don't let them get you angry. Don't yell back.

CONCHITA: Right.

They all start to exit.

SONIA: Sara, let's go.

SARA: I don't think so.

SONIA: We need you to help us.

SARA: I don't care if her panties are on the street.

CLARA: How can you say that?

SARA: She left. She didn't care what happened to her people, to her country. She went to live with the imperialists.

CUSA: You're a Communist.

SARA: I want everyone to be equal.

CUSA: So do I. So does everyone.

SARA: No. You just want to live like this forever. You don't want to share anything.

MIRIAM: You *are* a Communist!

CLARA: And you're still working for us?

CONCHITA: She's just repeating what she heard on the streets. Don't take her seriously.

SARA: I believe it. I trust them.

SONIA: And you don't trust us?
SARA: No.
MIRIAM: Then get the Communists to pay you.
SONIA: I thought I was your friend. Aren't we friends?
SARA: I'm a servant.

Exit Cusa and Miriam.

CONCHITA: Your mother is going to be so ashamed of you, Sara. Sarita. (*She exits*)
CLARA: You ungrateful slut. (*She exits*)
SARA: I hope she has to scrub for the rest of her life.
SONIA: I don't treat you like a servant. I've always been kind. Don't you trust *me*?

Sara stares at her.

SARA: No. Not really.

Exit Sonia, running. Pedro enters from the kitchen. He is carrying bottles of rum. He tries to pick up a stack of records from the coffee table. He drops a bottle.

PEDRO: Help me.
SARA: No, I have to go.
PEDRO: Help me with the records.
SARA: I told them a story.
PEDRO: What kind?
SARA: About the truth. And they didn't like it.
PEDRO: Who can blame them? You know, as I was crossing the hall, I thought I heard Fabiola laugh. She was laughing at me, believe me.
SARA: She's not there.
PEDRO: She's intact!
SARA: She's dead!
PEDRO: They're coming.

He starts to exit. "The Internationale" begins to play outside. He turns.

Was it funny?
SARA: What?
PEDRO: The story.
SARA: No.
PEDRO: Then why tell it?

Exit Sara. Pause. Exit Pedro. Enter Cusa, Miriam, Clara, carrying torn photographs, panties and bras. They throw them on top of the roses.

CLARA: They threatened to shoot.
CUSA: They won't.

Pedro enters the upstairs room. He opens a bottle and begins to drink.

CLARA (*Downstairs*): I'll bet they sent for that truck.
CUSA: Let's go back.
MIRIAM: Till every belonging is off the street.

Exit Miriam and Cusa.

CLARA: They're going to tell people. It's so humiliating.

She starts to cry. "The Internationale" grows louder.

Scene 3

Afternoon. The ballroom. Sonia and Conchita are embroidering. Sonia is eight months pregnant.

SONIA: I'm ashamed to arrive at Miami Beach in 1961 wearing clothes from 1954. Everything's changed so much.
CONCHITA: Your husband and son will be glad to get you no matter what you're wearing.
SONIA: I hope so.
CONCHITA: I'm certain.
SONIA: I wonder what color bath towels Osvaldo bought. And if we have dishes, do they match? Clara wrote me that her house was furnished with what other people didn't want, that nothing matched, not the towels or the dishes or the sheets. And Conchita, Miriam wrote me that they don't have bidets.
CONCHITA: How do they keep clean?
SONIA: I don't know.
CONCHITA: Miriam is there. Raulito. Your son. You'll feel at home.
SONIA: Clara is there too. (*Pause*) She had to start working in a factory; Ricardo wasn't making enough.
CONCHITA: Osvaldo will provide for you.
SONIA: I'd be too afraid. (*She holds up a handkerchief*) Is this good?
CONCHITA: Beautiful. Osvaldo will love it.

Enter Alfredo. He is carrying a briefcase.

ALFREDO: They kept looking at the briefcase. I was afraid they would search it but they just stared.

CONCHITA: What did you find?

ALFREDO (*Opening the case*): Three pounds of pork.

SONIA: How delicious.

ALFREDO: Twenty-five dollars.

CONCHITA: Sweet Christ!

ALFREDO: I could have bargained but I was too afraid of being caught. (*He continues*) Two pounds of rice, ten dollars; two pounds of shrimp, fifteen dollars; one pound of coffee, eight dollars; a pound of sugar, six dollars.

CONCHITA: I'll cook fried pork tonight, shrimp tomorrow.

ALFREDO: Good. (*He takes out a pint of whiskey*)

CONCHITA: Why that?

ALFREDO: A pint of whiskey, fifty dollars. He needs it to relax.

SONIA: They tried again this morning.

ALFREDO: Yes?

SONIA (*Shakes her head*): She's lucky she's dead. God was on her side. She never had to live through these last five years. She's lucky to have died. I keep hoping I'll wake up and find out it's 1953; that would be a relief.

Enter Cusa. Alfredo hands her the whiskey.

CUSA: You found it. Thank God.

ALFREDO: He needs it, I get it. Is it over at the cemetery?

CUSA: Still the same. Her fingernails look manicured. I looked a moment; Pedro just cried. Her aunt asked if we could put her back into our mausoleum.

CONCHITA: Did you put the crucifix inside?

CUSA: I gave it to the gravedigger. I let him do it.

CONCHITA: Did he put it in?

CUSA: Yes.

CONCHITA: She'll be dust in a little box soon.

CUSA: Let's hope.

ALFREDO: Pedro?

CUSA: I gave him three sedatives. He's asleep in my room.

SONIA: We should hold a mass for her.

FABIOLA

CONCHITA: The cross will do it.

SONIA: I'll do a rosary tonight.

Pause.

CUSA: It's so quiet.

CONCHITA: No children. No shooting.

SONIA: They stopped playing "The Internationale."

ALFREDO: Time for my afternoon nap.

SONIA: Sweet dreams.

ALFREDO: I'll try. (*He exits*)

CUSA: When I saw her looking like she was alive, I said to myself: "She's been dead since 1954?" At that moment I understood. I knew why it was a curse.

SONIA: Who cursed us? Why curse us?

CUSA: We sinned.

SONIA: Against what?

CUSA: Our country. We didn't love it enough.

SONIA: We.... It's too confusing now. I need to relax.

CUSA: I spent my life with my mind full of secrets. I always left the room when my father was discussing business. But I would try to hear what he was saying while I stood on the other side of the door, praying he wouldn't find me. I tried to help my country. But I kept my windows closed so no one could hear me. Thinking that by thinking it, it would be so.

SONIA: Oh...

CUSA: But I stayed the same. And I did nothing.

SONIA: I was taught on what side the knife should be, what side the fork, how to waltz, how to butter my bread little piece by little piece, that you must have good penmanship, how to embroider, to be a good Catholic, to be kind to people who work for you, to have faith, to honor my husband, to obey my father...

CONCHITA (*Looking at Sonia's embroidery*): That's such a beautiful stitch: a perfect O.

SONIA: What good is it going to do me in a country where they don't even have bidets?!

CUSA: Sonia, you have to go. We have to escape, little by little, each one of us. Fidel wants a country where we don't belong.

SONIA: I will always remember how to make floating islands. First you make an egg custard with milk, cornstarch, and three eggs. And a teaspoon of vanilla, of course. Then the syrup: a cup of sugar to two cups of water, and brandy to taste. While it's cooking you make the meringue: two tablespoons of sugar to each egg white and a little cream of tartar so they stay firm and fluffy. I know how to make them the right consistency so they stay firm. When the syrup starts to boil, you throw in the custard, one spoonful at a time. Then you put a spoonful of meringue on top. If you're lucky they'll float. Little islands, like Key Biscayne. I can always get them to float.

Sonia starts to cry. Enter Pedro. He sits by Sonia and watches as she resumes her embroidery.

Pedro, I'm sorry.

CUSA: Don't talk about it.

SONIA: I'm sorry, Cusa. Every stitch in and out. The nuns taught me how to embroider. They were so strict; that's why I'm so good at it. They were never pleased. (*Pause*) Pedro, remember Fabiola and me? Both of us pregnant, sitting on the porch sipping cokes?

PEDRO: Embroidering?

SONIA: Yes. On the front porch.

PEDRO: Embroidering little flowers out of silk thread onto tiny tops and cotton pants for babies.

SONIA: Yes, we grew up together. And tomorrow I'll go and when I'll see you again, I'll never know. Isn't that scary? (*Pause*) The first time we talked was my coming-out party. You were my partner because my mother said you danced better than Osvaldo, remember? What fun! We waltzed and then we did a rhumba, and then to show that we were up-to-date we did the boogie woogie.

CUSA: Would you like a little bit of food?

CONCHITA: I'm making pork tonight.

SONIA: And the times we swam all the way out to Hemingway's yacht, and that one time his sons threw all the furniture overboard. . . . My father knew they were crazy; they were nuts. But I loved playing practical jokes. . . . You and Osvaldo once ordered a case of champagne and a birthday cake.

PEDRO: A case of brandy. We drank it, just me and him alone.

SONIA: You also ordered a roast leg of pork and a paella from La Terasa. You had it all delivered to the people across the street. They had to give a party, and they never suspected you and Osvaldo were the ones.

FABIOLA

PEDRO: When you danced you looked sexy.

SONIA: Not in front of your mother!

PEDRO: Osvaldo used to say you were the Cuban Rita Hayworth.

SONIA: Pedro, don't embarrass me.

PEDRO: It's true. That's what he thought. We told each other things.

CUSA: Private things that brothers talk about, secrets between men, should not be told to mothers and wives.

PEDRO: Does he tell you about me, in your letters?

SONIA: He asks about you sometimes.

PEDRO: Did he tell you that he loved me?

SONIA: I know he loves you; you're his brother. What a silly thing to say.

PEDRO: He wants to hide from me.

SONIA: Why would he, Pedro? That's not true.

PEDRO: He's ashamed.

SONIA: Pedro, you're brothers; he loves you. He could never be ashamed.

PEDRO: Sonia, she knew. . .

CUSA: Your father found some. Want a sip?

PEDRO: Fabiola knew.

CUSA: To relax you. (*She pours him a drink*)

PEDRO: When you go, give me his letters.

SONIA: No.

PEDRO: So I can feel like he's around.

SONIA: The letters are personal; I wouldn't want you to read them.

PEDRO: We had no secrets.

SONIA: But we did!

CUSA: Drink. (*She hands him a glass*)

PEDRO: Why doesn't he write me?

SONIA: He doesn't want to see you suffering.

PEDRO: He's not here!

CUSA: You can have my letters.

PEDRO: When you see him, tell him to forgive me. That it made everything a mess.

SONIA: What?

PEDRO: Don't forget about the letters.

Exit Pedro followed by Cusa.

SONIA: He scares me.

CONCHITA: He's lost. Poor baby.

SONIA: That's why Osvaldo ignored him, I know. Osvaldo tried to help but Pedro wanted him around all the time. That's why Osvaldo ignored him. I know he scares him too. (*She embroiders*) Fabiola: that's why he went crazy. Fabiola.

Scene 4

The upstairs room. Pieces of letters are neatly taped to a glass closet. Pedro, in bed, begins to awaken.

PEDRO: Osvaldo. . .aahhhhhhhhhhh. . . . She is dust, finally. . .outside in the sun for a day. . .she blew away.

He stands, drinks some rum, crosses to the closet and begins to read the letters.

"July 11, 1967, Mama y Papa, we bought a forty-five-thousand-dollar house with five bedrooms. Nothing like Cuba, but nice. We're going to build a pool. It's on a hillside. In the United States the poor live on the flatland, the rich on the hill; the opposite of Cuba, isn't it funny?" (*Pause*) She turned to dust; you weren't there. "November 18, 1962, Mama y Papa, we miss you so. I'm working now in a car lot, washing cars. My hands get cold. All my love, Osvaldo." (*Pause*) I loved you more than anyone, my little brother. Not temporary, always.

In the kitchen Alfredo is smoking a cigarette. Enter Cusa, with a suitcase.

ALFREDO: I'm going to go there and live quietly and happily.
CUSA: Without the actress.
ALFREDO: I've given her up.

Pause. Enter two milicianos.

MILICIANO 1: Alfredo Marquez. Concepsion Marquez.
ALFREDO: Yes.
MILICIANO 1: Pedro Marquez.
CUSA: Upstairs.
MILICIANO 1: We will take inventory. If everything is the same as in the original inventory, then you will be given your visas for the USA. I'll do the living room and upstairs room; you, the rest.

Exit both milicianos.

FABIOLA

CUSA: I can't let them touch my things.

ALFREDO: We have to let them.

CUSA: I don't want to watch them do it.

Miliciano 1 enters the upstairs room. Pedro is on the bed.

MILICIANO 1: I'm taking inventory of the property. We are checking the whole house. You'll be leaving today.

PEDRO: Leaving?

MILICIANO 1: Hiding in the USA.

PEDRO: My brother lives in Los Angeles.

MILICIANO 1 (*Taking inventory*): One: mirrored closet. Two: desk. Three: vanity. Four: nightstand. Five: bed. Is this where you brought your maids?

PEDRO: No, this was the fuck room.

MILICIANO 1: That's what I mean. In this room you raped your maids or bought them with dollars.

PEDRO: It was the honeymoon room, that's all.

MILICIANO 1: Silver comb. Silver mirror. I bet. Perfume bottle. Silk bedspread. Cotton sheet.

PEDRO: It was a place where I loved someone.

MILICIANO 1: While the rest of us starved.

PEDRO: On a hillside? (*He begins to disrobe*) In the U.S. the poor live on the flatland, the rich on the hill. Isn't it funny? (*He is naked*) Let me stay. Make me part of the inventory. I am part of this room.

MILICIANO 1: Who would feed you?

PEDRO: The revolution?

MILICIANO 1: We have nothing to give to people like you. (*He looks Pedro over*)

PEDRO: Would you like to? Here.

MILICIANO 1: What?

PEDRO: Me. Anything you want of me. Remember what they used to say?

MILICIANO 1: When?

PEDRO: Back then. When I caught that big swordfish.

MILICIANO 1: They used to say you were one of *those*. And you are.

PEDRO: They used to say a hole's a hole and no real man would turn one down.

Pause.

MILICIANO 1: All right. That'll be it. No kissing and I don't want you to come over my clothes.

PEDRO: I won't.

Miliciano 1 undoes his belt. Pedro turns. Miliciano 1 touches his back.

Like going to a whore, but safer.

MILICIANO 1: No talking.

PEDRO: Brother.

MILICIANO 1: Shut up!

Pedro turns and kisses him on the lips. Miliciano 1 hits him in the stomach and Pedro falls back on the bed.

You're a worm. You're rotting. That's why Cuba is rotting, because of people like you.

PEDRO: You're right. It was our fault. We drank champagne and brandy; you starved.

Miliciano 1 slaps him.

MILICIANO 1: You think you're so superior. You went to private schools. I used to beg Americans for pennies while you drove around in your European cars. (*He starts to exit*)

PEDRO: I'll beg.

Exit Miliciano 1. Pedro goes to the record player, puts on a record: Nat King Cole singing "Sentimental Reasons." Pedro walks into the bathroom. In the kitchen Cusa and Alfredo wait. Enter the two milicianos.

MILICIANO 1: Check the suitcase. Only two changes of clothes each.

Miliciano 2 rummages through the suitcase.

MILICIANO 2: Two dresses, two bras, two panties, two stockings. . . . Four pairs of man's underwear?

ALFREDO: Two are for my son.

MILICIANO 1: Right.

MILICIANO 2: Four pairs of pants. . .shirts. . .an envelope.

MILICIANO 1: What's in it?

CUSA: Photos. Photos of my old farm, photos of my old car, photos of my old house.

MILICIANO 2: Photos. Should we let them take the photos?

MILICIANO 1: It's against the rules.

CUSA: Take them. I don't need photos to remember.

FABIOLA

Miliciano 2 puts the photos on the table. He closes the suitcase.

MILICIANO 1: The keys.

Alfredo hands him the keys. Exit Alfredo, running.

CUSA: In 1945 Pedro and Osvaldo had asthma attacks. The doctor said we needed to be near the beach. The first house I bought was haunted; we saw furniture move around. Two children had died in that house of scarlet fever in 1886. Their fever got so high they started to burn up and they screamed all night long before they died in 1886.

Pedro enters the upstairs room. His face is full of shaving cream. He picks up a straight razor.

It was their ghosts we heard every night. I got my children out of that house. This house was built by an ambassador from Spain. He assured me that no one had died here; the gypsy said it was true.

MILICIANO 1: The history of the Marquezes, hmmm.

MILICIANO 2: Shhhh.

CUSA: I bought this place in 1945 for cash, my father's money. Only one person died here. Fabiola, June 11, 1954. The house was free of ghosts till '54.

MILICIANO 1: Lady?

Pedro slices his wrist with the razor. Blood pours out.

CUSA: Yes.

MILICIANO 1: Get out.

CUSA: Yes, I am going. (*She starts to exit; shouting*) Pedro! It's time!

PEDRO (*Upstairs*): Aren't we fighting back?

CUSA: When I come back.

Exit Cusa. Pedro lies on the bed.

MILICIANO 2 (*Downstairs*): So this is where they had the big parties.

MILICIANO 1: They had no morals. None.

MILICIANO 2: I used to wash their cars.

MILICIANO 1: My wife wants me to sneak her in here tonight. She says it will be like staying at the Hilton.

END OF PLAY

IN THE EYE OF THE HURRICANE

CHARACTERS

MANUELA, lady of the house
MARIA JOSEFA, her mother
MARIO, her brother
OSCAR, her husband
SONIA, her daughter
HUGO, her orphaned nephew
ROSA, her maid
ANTONIO, her cousin
FULGENCIO, a bus driver
MILICIANO 1
MILICIANO 2

TIME

Act One: a spring day, 1960.
Act Two: the following day.

PLACE

Guanabacoa, Cuba.

IN THE EYE OF THE HURRICANE

ACT ONE

Scene 1

*A dining room. A large mahogany table, modern in style, many chairs
around it. Ledgers stacked on the table. A sideboard. Doors leading
to a tropical garden. Beyond it, the field where the buses are kept. Next
to the field, the garage. Yet all we see on stage is the furniture and doors
upstage center.*

Mario runs in, Maria Josefa follows him.

MARIA JOSEFA: Let me read it.

MARIO: No!

MARIA JOSEFA: Come on, read it to your mother. I'm your mother.

MARIO: I'll tear it up before I let you read it!

MARIA JOSEFA: You shouldn't keep secrets from your mother.

MARIO: I'm forty-five years old.

MARIA JOSEFA: Come on, son. You're fifty. Don't lie about your age to your
   mother. You're fifty!

MARIO: I was born in 1908.

MARIA JOSEFA: One nine zero eight from 1960 is fifty-two. You're fifty-two.

MARIO: Mama!

MARIA JOSEFA: Believe me, I remember when I gave birth to you. I have
   a daughter who's already in her sixties; she lies about her age also.

MARIO: All right, I'm fifty-two, more reason that you should give me a little bit of privacy and not try to read my mail.

MARIA JOSEFA: Which tart wrote you this one?

MARIO: None of your business.

MARIA JOSEFA: The last one...

MARIO: Shut up!

MARIA JOSEFA: Never married, that's the tragedy of your life.

Rosa enters.

ROSA: Here it is, the treat.

MARIA JOSEFA: Now that's a good girl.

Mario exits.

Where are you going? Never answers me.

Rosa hands her a glass of lemonade. Maria Josefa drinks.

Yum, lemonade, bitter and sweet.

ROSA: I just like the sweet part.

MARIA JOSEFA: That's why you're the maid and I'm the employer.

ROSA *(Hurt)*: Maria Josefa?!

MARIA JOSEFA: Don't be hurt. It's a fact, the only way to be successful in life is to enjoy the… *(She falls asleep)*

ROSA: What?

MARIA JOSEFA *(Coming back)*: …bittersweet.

ROSA: Success.

MARIA JOSEFA: Lemonade.

ROSA: Fidel Castro, he's the most successful man in Cuba.

MARIA JOSEFA: For now.

ROSA: Your daughter likes him, she thinks he's a hero.

MARIA JOSEFA: Just because she thinks it doesn't mean I agree.

ROSA: It's hard working here. I don't know who to be loyal to.

MARIA JOSEFA: Be loyal to me, you're in my will.

ROSA: One feels safe when you have one person who's the boss. I thought Mr. Hernandez was it—that would have been easy—but Mario, he's so—

MARIA JOSEFA: Careful! Remember he's my son. He's my son.

ROSA: I like him. I'm used to him. The cleaning lady doesn't like him. He's always ordering her around.

MARIA JOSEFA: With Mario, ordering is a need, not an obligation.

ROSA: And you and your daughter are always in conflict about dinner plans.

MARIA JOSEFA: Listen to what I tell you and you'll be fine.

ROSA: I've been working here now for ten years, I think I've figured out a way to survive—one just has to get by.

MARIA JOSEFA: "Getting by" is not enough, my dear. You have to be greedy. Sit down, relax and listen to me.

Manuela enters.

IN THE EYE OF THE HURRICANE

MANUELA: Rosa, the tomato sauce is burning.

ROSA: Oh no! Oh, my God! I'm so sorry. I got carried away talking.

MARIA JOSEFA: Talking to me, I'll go see if I can save it. (*She exits*)

MANUELA: Mama, let Rosa.

ROSA: I'm so sorry.

MANUELA: Go and help her. She's not strong enough to be cooking. What's this? Lemonade. With sugar. I told you to be strict about—

ROSA: It's hard. She doesn't know how sick—

MANUELA: But you know how sick she is. I've explained it to you.

ROSA: But I feel sorry for your mother. She—

MANUELA: Don't manipulate me.

ROSA: But she manipulates me.

MANUELA: Don't let her.

ROSA: Not so easy, I have a kind heart.

MANUELA: I have to finish last night's accounts. Try to get her to take some medicine.

ROSA: Fine.

MANUELA: Take her out to the patio.

ROSA: Fine.

MANUELA: Don't burn anything else.

ROSA: Fine.

Rosa exits. Manuela sits down and goes through the ledgers.

MANUELA (*To herself, sighs*): I feel safe here in my dining room. It is my domain.

Maria Josefa enters.

MARIA JOSEFA: What, dear?

MANUELA: I was just...

MARIA JOSEFA: Just what?

MANUELA: Talking to myself.

MARIA JOSEFA: Talking to yourself? That's a bad sign, dear. That's the beginning of a deteriorating mind, and a deteriorated mind leads to a collapsing body... (*She wanders off*)

MANUELA: Mama, what? Finish what you are saying.

Pause.

MARIA JOSEFA: My father talked to himself. So did my husband and look what happened to them.

MANUELA: What happened to them, what?!

MARIA JOSEFA: They died.

MANUELA: Not of natural causes. Neither one of them died of natural causes, Mama.

MARIA JOSEFA: What's the difference.

MANUELA: Their deaths were violent. Fate. Accidental.

MARIA JOSEFA: Accidents? May God forgive them for their accidents.

MANUELA: Then Mama, how could it have anything to do with their minds deteriorating, 'cause they talked to themselves? When they didn't have deaths caused by sickness. They didn't have normal deaths.

MARIA JOSEFA: So?

MANUELA: Their deaths had nothing to do with their mental or physical condition.

MARIA JOSEFA: Maybe.

MANUELA: Sometimes a person has a thought, and in order for that thought, idea, to become real, you have to say it aloud.

MARIA JOSEFA: So what was this great thought?

MANUELA: Never mind.

MARIA JOSEFA: I want to hear it, Mama wants to hear it.

MANUELA: I said, "I feel safe here in my dining room. It is my domain."

MARIA JOSEFA: See, I'm right. You're in trouble. One foot in the grave. Feeling safe. How can a woman feel safe?

MANUELA: You're so pessimistic, Mama. (*She puts some of the ledgers inside the sideboard and locks it*)

MARIA JOSEFA: Feeling safe means that you are tempting fate, playing with disaster. Dangerous to feel safe, Manuela. It leads you right into violence and death.

MANUELA: Safety?!

MARIA JOSEFA: Yes.

MANUELA: Mama!

MARIA JOSEFA: Believe me.

MANUELA: Oh, Mama. Please... (*She lights a cigarette*)

MARIA JOSEFA: Give me one.

Manuela gives her a cigarette.

A puff from a cigarette. Now that's a sensation.

IN THE EYE OF THE HURRICANE

MANUELA: If I can't feel safe in my own dining room, then where?

MARIA JOSEFA: The only thing that makes me feel safe is counting money. Counting, adding, seeing the result. Profit, safety. Let me count.

MANUELA: I already counted last night's take. Too bad for you.

MARIA JOSEFA: Did you make the deposit yourself?

MANUELA: Yes.

MARIA JOSEFA: Good.

MANUELA: Oh, God!

MARIA JOSEFA: What?

MANUELA: I got a cramp in my calf.

MARIA JOSEFA: I don't feel sorry for you.

MANUELA: God does it hurt.

MARIA JOSEFA: No sympathy from me.

MANUELA: Who's asking you for sympathy?

MARIA JOSEFA: It's because of that exercise bike you bought yourself. A bicycle that goes nowhere, you just sit and pedal, like a moron. Who ever heard of a woman in her sixties exercising?

MANUELA: Gringos.

MARIA JOSEFA: I never thought you'd grow up to be so vain.

MANUELA: Smart, not vain. It's beginning to go away.

MARIA JOSEFA: Going to the saunas was bad enough, then dyeing your hair.

MANUELA: I like Oscar to keep interested in me.

MARIA JOSEFA: If you want to keep your husband interested, learn how to be a better cook.

MANUELA: The maids cook well enough...

MARIA JOSEFA: Give a man a special kind of seasoning when you cook. The right spices that make up your own special flavor. That's what men want from their wives. 'Specially by the time they are sixty.

MANUELA: Fifty-nine.

MARIA JOSEFA: What a vain girl you grew up to be. That taste that he can only get at home, that's what you should—

MANUELA: You've managed to depress me, and I was feeling so...

MARIA JOSEFA: Sure?

MANUELA: Rub my leg.

MARIA JOSEFA: It's a curse to get old.

MANUELA: I'm not old yet, not inside, still look all right outside.

MARIA JOSEFA: That's because you haven't had any disappointment.

MANUELA: I'm disappointed that you refuse to rub my leg.

MARIA JOSEFA: I want another cigarette.

Manuela lights her another and one for herself.

True disappointment with life, that's the curse that brings old age.
You've never been disappointed so you think you're young.

MANUELA: Maybe I'll never know disappointment. Maybe I'll stay young
forever. Things now are—

MARIA JOSEFA: Going to get better?

MANUELA: Yes.

MARIA JOSEFA: I've never trusted men with beards.

MANUELA: It's only a trademark.

MARIA JOSEFA: They look like they don't bathe.

MANUELA: He'll be more honest than—

MARIA JOSEFA: Don't you dare say a word against Batista!

MANUELA: Never mind.

Maria Josefa looks out the doors. Manuela looks over the accounts.

MARIA JOSEFA: One of the lilies of the valley has come out to look at me.

MANUELA: It's too early in the year for lilies to bloom. They're still little
plants. In a month—

MARIA JOSEFA: No, look over there. *(She points out the door)* You see it now,
sweetheart.

MANUELA: It's early, it's an early riser, that one.

MARIA JOSEFA: Flowers don't know about time.

MANUELA: Well, maybe not time, but cycles, seasons.

MARIA JOSEFA: No, I don't think so. I think they just are. Once a whole
field of lilies of the valley bloomed for me. You don't believe me? But
they did! It's when we lived in a much more rural part of town,
Guanabacoa was much more rural then, than now. More open fields,
and we lived next to a huge field. It was the night before my first communion, I had been fasting all day, so I could be clean when the Sacred
Sacrament entered my body.

Maria Josefa lights a cigarette. Pause.

MANUELA: And?

MARIA JOSEFA: What...?

MANUELA: Did you fall asleep?

MARIA JOSEFA: The day before my first communion?

IN THE EYE OF THE HURRICANE

MANUELA: No, just now.

MARIA JOSEFA: And it bloomed, a field full of lilies, and I knew the Holy Sacrament wanted me. (*She laughs*) Wanted me, that was the last moment I ever had in my life that was simple. And today "He" only shows me one.

MANUELA: Maybe it's not just for you.

MARIA JOSEFA: I know I'm dying.

MANUELA: What are you talking about, Mama?

MARIA JOSEFA: I asked him to let me know, how long, how much more.

MANUELA: You should rest before lunch.

MARIA JOSEFA: Take me to my room.

MANUELA: Yes.

MARIA JOSEFA: Read me last night's figures.

MANUELA: Yes. (*She takes the ledgers*)

MARIA JOSEFA: Make a profit?

MANUELA: Of course.

MARIA JOSEFA: Busier than usual?

MANUELA: Yes. Rosa!

ROSA (*Entering*): Yes?

MANUELA: Bring me Mama's medicine.

Manuela and Maria Josefa exit.

ROSA: When will I get a moment's rest.

Rosa sits and closes her eyes. Mario enters; he has a pocket watch, he looks at the time and then begins to flip it in his hand.

MARIO: On break?

ROSA: You timing me?

MARIO: With this. . . . See, gold, heavy, feel it.

ROSA: Leave me alone.

MARIO: Solid, heavy, strong like me.

ROSA: Dense. Like your mind. Always ticking away.

MARIO: Dense, no. Intricate, full of levers to keep it running.

ROSA: Evil.

MARIO: I've never taken advantage of you, never once pinched your butt.

ROSA: You never once looked at my tits.

MARIO: So what?

ROSA: There's something wrong with a man that doesn't look at my tits.

MARIO: Maybe I have manners, taste.

ROSA: Never knew a man who didn't notice my—

MARIO: Breast! Don't say "tits," "breast."

ROSA: You're the only man who's never looked at them.

MARIO: Show them to me now.

ROSA: No!

MARIO: Now's your chance.

ROSA: Your mother's medicine, I have to take it to her.

MARIO: Let me admire them.

ROSA: Evil.

MARIO: Let me see, show me.

ROSA: You're supposed to sneak a look, I'm not supposed to exhibit them in front of you. One little look when I'm not looking. (*She exits*)

MARIO: Sneak a look? I'm supposed to enjoy seeing your blubbery boobs by sneaking a look? Nationalize? Bullshit! Nationalize. Fuck you, God!

Hugo enters.

HUGO: Were you calling me?

MARIO: No.

HUGO: I heard you yelling out.

MARIO: I was cursing God, not calling you.

HUGO: Sorry.

Mario grabs Hugo's arm.

MARIO: Fight me.

HUGO: I don't feel like it.

MARIO: Come on, show me your strength.

HUGO: All right.

They start to arm-wrestle. Mario twists Hugo's arm.

MARIO: See?

HUGO: All right! Please stop! You won! You win!

MARIO: That's right, I won.

HUGO: You're stronger than me, so what?

MARIO: You better get strong.

HUGO: I will. (*He exits*)

MARIO: Some things, I win. I'm going to outlive you, Maria Josefa.

He begins to weep. Manuela enters.

IN THE EYE OF THE HURRICANE

MANUELA: You're crying, Mario.
MARIO: Leave me alone.
MANUELA: What is it?
MARIO: I got a cold.
MANUELA: How did you get it?
MARIO: I don't know, how does one get anything. . .
MANUELA: By working for it.

Mario laughs.

MARIO: Really, is that how?
MANUELA: Don't be sarcastic.
MARIO: You seem to know so much, sister.
MANUELA: What are you implying?
MARIO: Nothing, I'm stuffed up, out of. . .
MANUELA: Out of what?
MARIO: Place, out of place.
MANUELA: Well. . .
MARIO: It's Mama.
MANUELA: Yes.
MARIO: Her illness. What's it called again?
MANUELA: Diabetes.
MARIO: Have you told her yet?
MANUELA: I'm not going to tell her.
MARIO: That sugar, all that sweet sugar water is killing her. The syrup she
    has for blood has gone out of control. (*He starts to cry*)
MANUELA: Everyone thinks that their mother will never die. I don't like
    seeing you sad.
MARIO: I'm crying from anger!
MANUELA: Never mind, Mario.
MARIO: Mother's illness has made me angry at you and your husband.
MANUELA: You're my brother and I've tried—
MARIO: Angry at you.
MANUELA: Tried to reach you, but—
MARIO: Your husband—
MANUELA: Stop your accusations.
MARIO: I haven't accused anybody.
MANUELA: We would have been nowhere, if Oscar hadn't come into my
    life. He saved all of us.
MARIO: All but Papa.

MANUELA: Please. It's not my fault that Mama has . . . . It's not my fault that Papa . . .

MARIO: Right, let's not bring it up.

MANUELA: Fine.

MARIO: Fine.

They embrace.

MANUELA: Lunch will be ready soon.

Mario looks out the window.

MARIO: Here he comes.

MANUELA: Who?

MARIO: Your husband.

Manuela looks out.

MANUELA: Look, see him. He has a bunch of gladioluses for Mama. Look at the way he's talking to Hugo. He reassures your nephew with a touch, how he takes care of your dead brother's son. How my husband has protected us, all of us. And you resent him?

MARIO: Right.

MANUELA: Go and say hello to Mama.

MARIO: I drove to the corner and bought her a carton of Lucky Strikes.

MANUELA: Here. (*She goes into a drawer, and takes out a syringe*) You inject her, she thinks you have a steadier hand.

MARIO: Where's the medicine.

MANUELA: Rosa has it.

MARIO: Lucky Strikes.

MANUELA: She'll like that. Steal me a pack.

MARIO: If she lets me. (*He exits*)

MANUELA: Hello, flowers for me?

OSCAR (*Offstage*): No.

MANUELA: I know—for my mother.

Oscar enters.

OSCAR: How can I?

MANUELA: How can you what?

OSCAR: Live without your mother.

MANUELA: We'll find a way.

IN THE EYE OF THE HURRICANE

OSCAR: I never had a mother.

MANUELA: Yes.

OSCAR: I thought that the only good thing about that was that I would never lose her, my mother.

MANUELA: And now you have to go through losing mine.

OSCAR: All of the pain and none of the ownership.

MANUELA: You're like a son to her.

OSCAR: But, not a son. "Like" is not the same thing as "He is my son," Mario is her son. Like being in cahoots with the new regime, doesn't mean that "you are" the new order.

MANUELA: Give Fidel a chance.

OSCAR: It's getting tougher.

MANUELA: Got the cash?

OSCAR: Sonia's surprise?

MANUELA: Yes!

OSCAR: Right, we're getting her a car today, right...

MANUELA: How could you forget?!

OSCAR: I didn't forget. It's in my pocket and ready. You know me. I like to tease you 'cause you're so stubborn.

MANUELA: I love you.

Hugo enters.

OSCAR: Look. (*He shows her an envelope with bills in it*)

HUGO: What is that?

MANUELA: We're getting Sonia her car.

HUGO: Lucky Sonia.

OSCAR: Don't be jealous. Doesn't pay to be jealous.

HUGO: I'm not jealous.

MANUELA: Good.

HUGO: Is it going to be a brand-new one?

OSCAR: Yes, of course.

HUGO: And she'll be the first person to smell it, smell the leather on the seats. And push down on the clutch and change gears.

MANUELA: Maybe when you get older, she'll let you drive it.

HUGO: When she gets bored with it—she gets bored with everything because she gets so much.

MANUELA: So do you. When you're older...

HUGO: Fidel will make sure I have a car.

MANUELA: Not like the one we're going to buy Sonia, it's English.

HUGO: You already picked it out for her.

OSCAR: I did. It's a beauty.

HUGO: Fidel wants everyone to have everything equally.

MANUELA: You believe that?

HUGO: Well, he does...

Mario enters.

MARIO: Fidel wants everyone to lose everything equally.

OSCAR: We're your family, Hugo, only family give each other things.

MANUELA: That's right. Listen to my husband.

HUGO: Everything for the family.

MANUELA: Everything for, from and in the family.

OSCAR: That's right. It's the only thing you can rely on, the only thing you can believe in.

HUGO: All right, how long do I have to wait for a car.

MANUELA: When Uncle decides that you've earned it.

HUGO: Uncle Oscar?

MARIO: Uncle Mario.

HUGO: Then I'll never see a car.

MARIO: You'll be driving a bus soon, like the rest of the family, so don't worry about cars.

MANUELA: No, he's going to school and become a foot specialist.

MARIO: A good profession for you.

HUGO: I'm going to talk to Grandma. Call when it's time for lunch.

MANUELA: Here, take her the gladioluses.

Hugo exits.

You tease him too much.

MARIO: I want him to be ready for it when it all falls apart.

MANUELA: What falls apart?

OSCAR: Get me some café. I need some café.

MANUELA: All right. I'll get Rosa to make it.

OSCAR: You make it better.

MANUELA: Not really.

OSCAR: For me you do.

MANUELA: All right. I've spoilt you.

OSCAR: I love it.

IN THE EYE OF THE HURRICANE

Manuela exits.

MARIO: You got up early today.
OSCAR: Had a lot of errands.
MARIO: Couldn't wait to have café with me, I guess...
OSCAR: Had a lot on my mind.
MARIO: Of course, so did I.
OSCAR: In the afternoon, we'll go to Havana, and have a couple of drinks...
MARIO: Maybe I needed to talk to you this morning. We got problems!
OSCAR: Is it the number five? Is it burning oil again? We're gonna have to rebuild the motor on that one...
MARIO: We bought it used, we should have bought a new one.
OSCAR: It was a bargain. Besides, you gotta trust a bus that drove on the streets of Chicago, Illinois, USA.
MARIO: It's running fine. It's a different dilemma we're facing.... It's hard to...
OSCAR: Who do you want to fire now?
MARIO: Nobody! Don't you see what's happening? Fidel is a Communist!
OSCAR: Fidel's no Communist. Don't start with that record again! Fidel's our boy! He got rid of Batista and that's all that matters.
MARIO: He conned us.
OSCAR: Shut up!
MARIO: So you did know about it. And you were not going to tell me?
OSCAR: It's only gossip.
MARIO: No it's not. I got a note today from Gilberto Valladares, my friend, who works in the Bureau of Information, for Fidel, where they write his speeches...
OSCAR: I want you to understand something. I want you to listen to me and understand one thing.... You know me well enough...
MARIO: Like a book. I know you like a book.
OSCAR: We are a couple of years away from being millionaires. From turning our beachfront property into a beautiful hotel. All my life I've wanted a beautiful hotel with a casino standing beside it. And a golf course adjoining it. And the Gulf of Mexico facing it, like a beautiful blue painting. All my life I've wanted to have a million dollars in my pocket. And no little rebellious punk is gonna cheat me out of my dreams!
MARIO: He already has.
OSCAR: Gossip. Mario the little gossip from—

MARIO: Oscar please, respect me.

OSCAR: Gossip from Guanabacoa.

MARIO: I have proof. And it spells out Communism.

OSCAR: No.

MARIO: Yes!

OSCAR: Trust me.

MARIO: Look at my eye. How it's been twitching, my upper lip, from nerves, I can't get it to stop.

OSCAR: What did Valladares send you?

MARIO: Feel my hands, cold, clammy, frightened.

OSCAR: Show me.

MARIO: Here it is.

Oscar reads.

It's a copy of a summons we're going to receive. . . . Are you panicked?

OSCAR: No, of course not. Did you tell your sister?

MARIO: No.

OSCAR: Good, we should protect her. . .

MARIO: From the truth?

OSCAR: Yes.

MARIO: Protecting is almost like lying, isn't it?

OSCAR: No, it's what men have to do.

MARIO: That's why I told you. I would never tell my sister.

OSCAR: She must never see that summons. Because it's not going to happen, they are not going to confiscate the buses. Have you told her about the note?

MARIO: I wanted to tell you first. We only have a few days to come up with some sort of plan to fight back. . .

Manuela enters.

MANUELA: The café.

OSCAR (*Taking a sip*): See. Delicious!

MANUELA: What were you two screaming about?

OSCAR: Usual stuff.

MARIO: Income.

MANUELA: I heard Mario scream that Fidel is a Communist. Rosa just heard on the radio that he's giving a speech tonight, to declare his intentions. I thought he declared his intentions when he was fighting

Batista. Has he found new ones? If he's a Communist, you know what that means?

OSCAR: What?

MANUELA: They don't believe in Christ. They don't believe in private ownership. I mean what is Fidel up to? You heard Hugo, that's dangerous talk.

OSCAR: This is a little country. What would Russia want with such a little country?

MANUELA: What they all want—a tan.

OSCAR: No, Russians live covered in snow. They're afraid of the sun. Mario, let's go.

MARIO: When will lunch finally be ready?

MANUELA: An hour.

MARIO: I'm hungry, tell her to hurry it up.

MANUELA: I will.

MARIO: Nervousness makes me want to eat.

MANUELA: Why are you so nervous?

OSCAR: Life—simple life makes your brother nervous. (*He exits*)

MANUELA: You would have been poor without him, you'd still be driving a bus.

MARIO: We might be poor again.

MANUELA: Never.

MARIO: You don't respect me, do you, sister?

MANUELA: I'm a woman who knows the only man that she can trust and respect is her husband.

MARIO: Here, don't say anything. I promised him, he told me not to show it to you, but you should know. I don't get nervous by simple life, I have a reason to be scared.

Mario hands Manuela the summons. She starts to read it. Blackout.

Scene 2

Lights up. Oscar is looking at the mirror. The note is in his hand.

OSCAR: Has someone disfigured my face? Why does my face feel crooked?

Manuela enters.

MANUELA: Is it true, the note...?

OSCAR: Mario's friends always exaggerate.

MANUELA: But is it true, Oscar?!

OSCAR: Yes, I think it's all true.

MANUELA: And you were trying to keep it from me.

OSCAR: Protect you.

MANUELA: I thought we were partners in this business, that I was an equal.

OSCAR: I thought that with your mother dying that you couldn't take any more . . .

MANUELA: I can take anything. I know how to fight.

OSCAR: I had forgotten that you're made out of steel.

MANUELA: And you like it.

OSCAR: I love it.

MANUELA: Who do we appeal to?

OSCAR: We don't know, he's going to announce it tonight. Then all the other bus companies together, we'll have a plan, a strike, a war. We'll win.

MANUELA: Do they want to buy them from us or what?

OSCAR: No, take, they want to take them.

MANUELA: Steal them.

OSCAR: They will be the nation's—nationalized.

MANUELA: Another word for stealing.

OSCAR: We'll still own them as part of the collective "we," as part of the national "we." That's his plan. But you know plans have a way of being interrupted.

MANUELA: You're so calm.

OSCAR: We'll find a solution, we have time.

MANUELA: Don't tell Mama.

OSCAR: I won't.

MANUELA: She doesn't have to know.

OSCAR: You look lovely today.

MANUELA: I had a facial.

OSCAR: Thank God for facials, then.

MANUELA: Tell me the plans? Do we try to protest, organize a way to overthrow him? God, why does everything in this country have to be so brutal?

Oscar puts his hand up Manuela's dress.

Oscar, answer me that, what does this country have against a ballot box?

IN THE EYE OF THE HURRICANE

OSCAR: Manuela.

MANUELA: We have to overthrow somebody else again.

OSCAR: Hmmmm, lovely.

MANUELA: Silk.

Oscar's hands are up Manuela's dress.

Expensive.

OSCAR: Thrilling.

MANUELA: That we can afford it?

OSCAR: That you still wear it so well.

MANUELA: Somebody might come in.

OSCAR: No.

MANUELA: Love me, don't you?

OSCAR: I want to keep touching, forever.

Manuela starts to laugh.

Still get excited, when I put my hand up your dress.

MANUELA: This is the first time you've ever done it.

OSCAR: No, before...

MANUELA: Never, not me. Must have been somebody else's dress you put your hands up, someone who could afford silk...

OSCAR: Never.

MANUELA: Really?

OSCAR: Yes...

MANUELA: Always been ready and available to you in our bed, you never had to sneak a touch with me, wealth allows a woman to stay younger...

OSCAR: Thank God.

MANUELA: My mother resents me, resents my appearance because she ended her sexual—her needs so early, she stopped being a woman at such an early age. Too soon.... And she thinks, knows, I'm still enjoying too much. Because of her struggles, so she resents the massages, the facial creams...

Oscar kisses her.

OSCAR: Us.

MANUELA: Yes, us. Let's take a siesta after lunch.

OSCAR: Let's forget.

MANUELA: Forget, no.

OSCAR: That it's daytime.

HUGO (*Entering*): Uncle Oscar, Mario needs you with him.

OSCAR: Now?!

MANUELA: Go, lunch is almost ready.

Oscar and Hugo exit. We hear a bus drive in. Manuela stands and looks out the doors. Rosa enters, sets the table.

ROSA: Looking at the garden? Is someone in it that's not supposed to be?

MANUELA: No, looking at the buses, the number eight just came in for its gasoline stop. On time, it's running on time today.

ROSA: How can you see the number from so far away?

MANUELA: I can't. I recognize the sound of the motor.

ROSA: They all sound the same to me.

MANUELA: Not to me. It's all I have.

ROSA: The buses?

MANUELA: Yes, they make me care.

ROSA: How about your husband, your daughter, your family?

Manuela starts to walk towards the garden. As she does, the dining room begins to dissolve.

MANUELA: I love them, but those buses are my reason, my future. My incentive, my job.

Rosa and Manuela exit. We are now inside a tool shed located in the field where the buses are kept. Mario is there with Antonio, who is eating a Cuban sandwich.

ANTONIO: You sure you don't want to sit where I'm sitting?

MARIO: Actually, I do.

ANTONIO: Sit—by all means—sit.

MARIO: I mean the chair is supposed to be for the management.

ANTONIO: Of course, perfectly understandable. I've been sitting all day long driving the bus anyway. I'm so glad I'm not the conductor anymore; that's a tough job, on your feet all day, having to deal with people all day.

MARIO: You have me to thank. I promoted you.

ANTONIO: Want a bite of my sandwich?

MARIO: No, I'm having lunch soon.

IN THE EYE OF THE HURRICANE

ANTONIO: I love the way cousin Manuela cooks. I might ask her to be the godmother to my baby, my wife wants her to be. My mother has missed the Sunday lunches. Will you be having one again soon, she wanted me to ask.

Oscar enters.

OSCAR: Tell your mother on Mother's Day as usual.

ANTONIO: Thank you, Oscar. Can't wait. Want a bite of my sandwich?

OSCAR: I need you to fill up the number ten.

ANTONIO: Right. Yes, sir. My wife and I were wondering if you and cousin Manuela would like to baptize our baby? You're the best godfather I could think of for my baby—we'd really like it. My mother said you already have so many that you've baptized half of Guanabacoa. . .

OSCAR: I would love to. Now go.

ANTONIO: Thank you, sir.

Antonio exits. Oscar goes to a box, unlocks it, and takes out a machine gun.

OSCAR: Why did you tell her?! Why do you always go behind my back?! Stop tricking me!

MARIO: She got it out of me. She knew already.

OSCAR: Liar!

MARIO: She tricked me.

OSCAR: Why? Haven't I been good to you? Haven't I treated you like a brother?

MARIO: You have.

OSCAR: Then why do you sabotage me?

MARIO: Because. . .

OSCAR: Because what?

MARIO: You overwhelm me.

OSCAR: You don't trust me.

MARIO: No, I don't.

OSCAR: From now on I give the orders and you follow. Understand?

MARIO: No. I have a right to give orders, also—to make decisions that concern us!

OSCAR: No, never!

MARIO: This is also mine!

OSCAR: When I let you, when I decide.

MARIO: No!

OSCAR: It's up to me!

MARIO: No more, no!

OSCAR: Don't fight me now, Mario, not now.

MARIO: Equal. I want it to be equal.

OSCAR: I'm the boss. (*He slaps Mario*) Understand?

MARIO: No.

Hugo enters.

HUGO: Wow, a machine gun. A real one.

OSCAR: Yes, real. Want to learn how to shoot it?

HUGO: Yeah. Yes. Shit, yes.

OSCAR: Let's go. I'll show you.

HUGO: Really, Uncle Oscar?

OSCAR: Really.

They start to exit.

Coming, Mario?

MARIO: When I'm ready.

OSCAR: I hope you're ready soon.

They exit. Mario tries not to follow Oscar, but then does. As Mario goes, we see Manuela with a bucket full of flowers she has been cutting. She enters the dining room. Rosa enters from the kitchen.

MANUELA: I want these flowers in the middle of the table.

ROSA: Is there enough room for flowers?

MANUELA: Yes, of course.

ROSA: It's important to you to look at flowers while you eat?

MANUELA: These ones I cut, take the bucket, put them in a vase.

ROSA: All right. (*She exits*)

MANUELA: I worked hard to be able to look at flowers when I eat. Worked hard to be able to do a lot of things. No one handed Oscar and me anything on any silver platter. . .

Rosa enters with the flowers.

ROSA: What?

MANUELA: I wasn't talking to you.

ROSA: Who's here?

IN THE EYE OF THE HURRICANE

MANUELA: Myself, God.

Rosa starts to arrange the flowers.

Leave me alone for a minute.

ROSA: But—

MANUELA: They look fine.

Rosa exits. Manuela takes a chair, sits, lights a cigarette, looks at the lighter.

Worked hard, didn't I? Aren't you supposed to reward people for honest work?

Maria Josefa enters.

MARIA JOSEFA: Starving. Light me one. One of mine, Lucky Strikes. I love American cigs.

Manuela hands her the lighter.

Silver, heavy.

MANUELA: Yes.

MARIA JOSEFA: Who did it belong to?

MANUELA: Father, don't you remember? All the headaches when you gave this to me?

MARIA JOSEFA: After he was shot.

MANUELA: Yes.

MARIA JOSEFA: Right. Mario accused me of, well, his usual accusations— was insulted that I gave it to you and not him.

MANUELA: Jealous.

MARIA JOSEFA: Yes, acted hurt. When is she going to have lunch ready?

MANUELA: Another half an hour she said.

MARIA JOSEFA: Lazy girl, that girl is so lazy.

MANUELA: You're the one that treats her like she's your best friend, makes her think she doesn't have to follow orders.

MARIA JOSEFA: I have a soft heart.

MANUELA: Well, how can one discipline a best friend?

MARIA JOSEFA: If it's in half an hour, why has she set the table already? The water will get warm. The ice cubes will melt. Help get these pitchers into the refrigerator.

MANUELA: It doesn't matter. I have to get some air. I'm suffocating. (*She runs out*)

MARIA JOSEFA: Silver lighter. . . . Warm water, cold food. That's what happens when you stop doing things for yourself.

Sonia enters.

SONIA: Is Mama all right?

MARIA JOSEFA: Aren't you going to give me a kiss?

SONIA: Mama looked like she was crying. Got angry at me and—

MARIA JOSEFA: Middle age, that's all.

SONIA: —screamed at me that I should help you keep the water cold.

MARIA JOSEFA: Forget it. It's useless to keep order in this house. Sit and talk to me.

SONIA: I'm hungry. When's lunch?

MARIA JOSEFA: Whenever Rosa feels like it.

SONIA: I thought I was late. I rushed here.

MARIA JOSEFA: No such thing as punctuality in this house. In and out, that's all. All day long, bus drivers, mechanics, friends. In and out. Why haven't they gotten an office?

SONIA: They wanted to keep it all with the family.

MARIA JOSEFA: "With the family" is different than in the house.

SONIA: Dad has an office for his other business.

MARIA JOSEFA: But still everything is handled out of this house, out of this dining room.

SONIA: Mama won't let go.

MARIA JOSEFA: Why should she? Neither will I. But I would have liked an office, a place to drive to, a desk. Counting money on the table where you eat corrupts the food. Pretty blouse.

SONIA: Thank you.

MARIA JOSEFA: The shorts, I don't approve of. What does your husband think about you crossing the street in these shorts?

SONIA: I haven't asked.

MARIA JOSEFA: Not ladylike.

SONIA: Grace Kelly wears shorts just like these and she's a princess.

MARIA JOSEFA: She was an actress first. Too short.

SONIA: Look at this handkerchief. Do you like it? The lettering?

MARIA JOSEFA: Now that's ladylike.

Rosa enters.

SONIA: Thank you. Hello, Rosa.

IN THE EYE OF THE HURRICANE

Rosa finishes setting the table.

ROSA: How's it look?

SONIA: Fine.

ROSA: Hmmm, smell something?

SONIA: What are we having?

ROSA: Shrimp with tomato, white rice.

SONIA: I like the way you make that.

MARIA JOSEFA: My recipe.

SONIA: Grandma!

MARIA JOSEFA: Isn't that right?

ROSA: Yes, of course. I have to make sure it doesn't burn. (*She exits*)

SONIA: Hmmmm.

MARIA JOSEFA: We'd sit with whole tablecloths, big ones, and embroider, my mother and me.

SONIA: How exciting.

MARIA JOSEFA: Restful, not exciting.

SONIA: Well, yes, exciting was the wrong word.

MARIA JOSEFA: Whole tablecloths we'd embroider for tables bigger than this one. People had larger families then, common to see a table that sat thirty. Easily.

SONIA: This one sits fifteen.

MARIA JOSEFA: Small, her on one side, me on the other.

SONIA: I wish. . .

MARIA JOSEFA: That you could have been there?

SONIA: That we still had one of those tablecloths so I could study it, maybe copy it. Maybe you could remember the stitch. And Mama, you and I could sit on the front porch and embroider one for this table.

MARIA JOSEFA: Too late.

SONIA: No.

MARIA JOSEFA: I don't remember the stitches, the pattern, just remember that it was beautiful and people envied us.

SONIA: It might all come back to you.

MARIA JOSEFA: We got too busy for those things, your mother and I. Then one forgets.

SONIA: I've learned how to at school, but small things, towels, handkerchiefs—

MARIA JOSEFA: Your work, it's lovely.

SONIA: Nothing as monumental as a tablecloth but—

MARIA JOSEFA: I feel seasick, that's old age. Feeling like you're on a rocky sea in a little boat that goes up and down, side to side, nothing stable, all the time, even on a clear, cool, still day like this one. Light the cig for me?

Sonia lights it.

Get one for yourself.

SONIA: I don't feel like it, thank you.

MARIA JOSEFA: Pregnant again?

SONIA: No.

MARIA JOSEFA: Never heard of a young woman turning down a cigarette.

SONIA: Don't feel like one now, that's all. The table looks pretty, the flowers could use more careful arranging.

MARIA JOSEFA: You know Rosa, throws things together carelessly.

SONIA: Doesn't have any pride.

MARIA JOSEFA: No, she doesn't have a work ethic.

SONIA (*Arranging flowers*): See, prettier, isn't it?

MARIA JOSEFA: Much.

SONIA: So hungry.

MARIA JOSEFA: Your husband?

SONIA: Having lunch at his mother's.

MARIA JOSEFA: Son?

SONIA: At school.

MARIA JOSEFA: So you have the whole afternoon to rearrange flowers, that's good.

SONIA: Papa and I are going to go shopping for a car.

MARIA JOSEFA: For whom?

SONIA: For me!

MARIA JOSEFA: For you?

SONIA: Yes.

MARIA JOSEFA: You've learned to drive?!

SONIA: Yes.

MARIA JOSEFA: How wonderful!

SONIA: I want a sports car, I think.

MARIA JOSEFA: Driving beats the hell out of embroidering.

They start to laugh.

SONIA: Maybe.

IN THE EYE OF THE HURRICANE

Manuela enters.

MANUELA: Sonia, go tell Rosa to start serving.

MARIA JOSEFA: You have a problem?

Sonia exits.

MANUELA: No.

MARIA JOSEFA: You've been talking and walking around for the last hour like somebody who has a problem.

MANUELA: Headache, hot.

MARIA JOSEFA: Still getting them?

MANUELA: Still.

MARIA JOSEFA: Our bodies are our curse.

MANUELA: And our blessing.

MARIA JOSEFA: More a curse than a blessing.

MANUELA: Still.

MARIA JOSEFA: What?

MANUELA: We have no choice.

MARIA JOSEFA: Better to have been born a man, believe me.

MANUELA: To have a man's body and a woman's intelligence, that's the winning combination. (*She looks out the door*) Here they come.

Sonia reenters.

SONIA: She's almost ready.

MANUELA: Rosa, they're coming up the garden, Rosa, hurry up, you know Mario likes his food hot.

ROSA (*Entering*): Burning, not just hot, burning! He doesn't think something is good unless it burns his tongue.

Sonia sits.

SONIA: Finally lunch.

MARIA JOSEFA: The men get served first.

SONIA: I know.

MARIA JOSEFA: We sit first, but they get served first.

MANUELA: She knows.

MARIA JOSEFA: Should I help you?

ROSA: Well.

MANUELA: No.

MARIA JOSEFA: Hugo coming for lunch?

MANUELA: He's with them.

Oscar, Mario and Hugo enter.

HUGO: Smells great!

ROSA: Shrimp and tomato. (*She enters and exits with food*)

MARIO: Great, who's going to serve me?

MARIA JOSEFA: I'll serve Oscar, Sonia, you serve your uncle...

HUGO: And me?

MANUELA: I will, nephew, it would be a pleasure.

ROSA: Here are some bananas.

MANUELA: Save some for yourself.

ROSA: Have a plate in the back.

OSCAR: Give me a kiss, sweetheart.

SONIA: Dad, well?

OSCAR: We'll have to see.

MANUELA: Don't tease her.

SONIA: I want something nice.

MARIA JOSEFA: A car.

MANUELA: Impressive, isn't it, Mama?

MARIA JOSEFA: Avocado for you, Oscar?

OSCAR: Two pieces.

MARIO: More, I'm starving.

SONIA: What else is new, Uncle?

HUGO: The bus drivers were acting strange today. One of them said goodbye.

Rosa exits to the front rooms.

SONIA: Maybe he's a Batistiano, maybe he's going to Miami to join the rest of them.

MANUELA: Yes, maybe.

MARIA JOSEFA: No talk against Batista in this house!

OSCAR: I'm beginning to miss Batista.

MARIA JOSEFA: How is it?

OSCAR: Good. Delicious.

MARIA JOSEFA: My recipe.

MANUELA: Oscar! Never mind. Mario, slow down when you're eating.

MARIO: I'm eating to keep myself from talking.

MANUELA: Then eat up!

MARIA JOSEFA: There's plenty more in the kitchen.

MANUELA: I know.

IN THE EYE OF THE HURRICANE

SONIA: And for the car.

OSCAR: Well...

SONIA: What kind of budget can I expect?

OSCAR: I took out what we can afford.

SONIA: Oh.

OSCAR: It's in my pockets.

SONIA: Oh.

OSCAR: A few bills.

SONIA: In your pocket?

OSCAR: Here, let's count it.

MANUELA: After lunch, surprises are better on a full stomach.

OSCAR (*Taking out bills*): One thousand.

SONIA: My God!

OSCAR: Two thousand.

MARIO: Two thousand dollars in two bills.

OSCAR: That's right.

MARIO: Let me, let me look at it.

SONIA: Let him keep counting!

MARIO: Pesos, a thousand pesos.

OSCAR: A peso is worth eleven cents more than a dollar.

MANUELA: So there!

MARIA JOSEFA: Let me see the other one.

OSCAR: Here you go.

SONIA: I want to hold them in my hands, all of them, however many there
are!

MARIA JOSEFA (*Looking at bill*): What beautiful pieces of paper.

SONIA: They're for me, for my car! (*She giggles*)

MANUELA: Give them back to her.

MARIO: Spoiled.

MARIA JOSEFA: I'm glad she's spoiled.

HUGO: Unbelievable, how much more, Uncle Oscar, how much more?!

OSCAR: It's only money. Now... (*Takes out more bills*) three thousand, four
thousand. For your new car.

SONIA: I'll be able to buy the sports car for sure now!

MANUELA: And keep the change.

HUGO: Let me hold it for a minute.

SONIA: No, it's mine. I love you, Papa. After lunch we'll go?

Rosa reenters from the front rooms.

ROSA: Sir, Mr. Oscar, there are three officials at the door.

OSCAR: We'll find the right car for you even if it takes all afternoon.

ROSA: Sir, I'm sorry to interrupt you, but three milicianos are at the front door. They have a document they want to give you. They wouldn't let me take it for you, they want you.

OSCAR: Tell them to wait till I'm through eating lunch.

ROSA: But sir. . .

OSCAR: Till I'm through eating lunch!

ROSA: Sir, madam, I'm scared of them.

MANUELA: I'll go talk to them.

Manuela and Rosa exit.

OSCAR: Tell them to wait till after lunch!

SONIA: It's going to be red, a Karmann Ghia maybe, an MG. Or a Fiat. If it's a Fiat, I want it to be white. I like Karmann Ghias, I think they're more roomy, more subtle. If it's a Karmann Ghia, I think gray. The color gray, MG dark green, Fiat, white, but all of them with a black leather interior. Hold my money, Daddy, till we buy it.

HUGO: Let me hold it.

SONIA: No! I'll hold it, it's mine!

MARIA JOSEFA: I can't eat this! It's choking me! Can't eat it! Rosa!

SONIA: I'll give you a ride in it, Hugo.

HUGO: Can I drive it? Will you let me?

SONIA: Only if I'm in the car with you.

OSCAR: Mario, I am finishing my lunch! We are finishing lunch!

MARIO: Fine, what difference does it make?

MARIA JOSEFA: Rosa!

Rosa enters.

ROSA: I'm here, I'm coming, they haven't left.

OSCAR: Tell Manuela to come and start eating her lunch. It's getting cold.

MARIA JOSEFA: Take me to my room. I'm feeling faint. I can't eat.

ROSA: Yes, hold on to me.

Maria Josefa and Rosa exit.

MARIA JOSEFA: Thank you, you're a sweet girl.

SONIA: Can I be excused from lunch, I can't eat, I can't wait, I have to go show Osvaldo.

IN THE EYE OF THE HURRICANE

MARIO: Go out the side door.

SONIA: Why?

MARIO: Just do it!

SONIA: All right.

OSCAR: Tell your husband, next car I expect him to pay for.

SONIA: He will. See you in a minute. (*She exits*)

OSCAR: Good shrimp, nice, Hugo, huh?

HUGO: Yes.

Manuela enters.

OSCAR: Now eat.

MANUELA: I don't want to.

OSCAR: Eat!

MANUELA: They read me the notice.

OSCAR: Not now, now we are eating.

MANUELA: They're taking them over after his speech tonight.

HUGO: What?

MANUELA: The buses.

MARIO: Let's burn them.

MANUELA: Never.

HUGO: What?

MANUELA: Fidel, he's getting rid of us.

HUGO: What?!

MANUELA: Leave the boy alone.

Maria Josefa runs in.

MARIA JOSEFA: One lily of the valley. It didn't mean one more year, one more month, it meant today, one more day for me to live.

MARIO: The old lady has gone crazy!

OSCAR: Shut up!

MARIA JOSEFA: My life.... Just today left. Hold me, Manuela, hold me.

Manuela goes toward Maria Josefa. Maria Josefa faints.

MANUELA: Fainted, don't go today, Mama, don't.

MARIO: Today, a day comes everything changes. Today.

OSCAR: No.

HUGO: Not everything.

OSCAR: I'll carry her to her room.

MANUELA: Yes.

HUGO: Not everything, Uncle Oscar!

Oscar and Manuela exit with Maria Josefa. Hugo starts to cry.

MARIO: Stop it. Eat.

HUGO: How can you think of eating?

MARIO: Why not?

HUGO: Pervert!

MARIO: Watch it?

HUGO: Old—

MARIO: Careful!

HUGO: Why should I be careful?

MARIO: Might tell.

HUGO: About what?

MARIO: We're all in the same boat.

HUGO: No.

MARIO: Did you get a hard-on when he was counting the money?

HUGO: Faggot. He got yours up.

MARIO: You need someone older to teach you.

HUGO: You?

MARIO: Do you?

HUGO: You would help me? Have you always been?

MARIO: What I do with my fluids is my business.

HUGO: Are you always watching me?

MARIO: What I do with my eyes is my business.

HUGO: Well, I don't want you.

MARIO: Arm-wrestle with me, and this time, try to win.

HUGO: All right. I will.

They start to arm-wrestle.

MARIO: There's happiness, when everybody loses, a sense of justice, a sense of peace, so make me lose.

HUGO: I'm trying.

MARIO: Try harder!

Blackout.

END OF ACT ONE

IN THE EYE OF THE HURRICANE

ACT TWO

Scene 1

The bus yard. On either side of the stage, there is the front of a bus. In the middle, open space. On the horizon, we see the garage. Late afternoon. Fulgencio, a man in his forties, and Antonio, in his twenties.

ANTONIO: Poor people.

FULGENCIO: They got quite a crowd.

ANTONIO: Father Beneficio passed out secret notes last night at the church.

FULGENCIO: I told every passenger last night to come and help the protest. First, they'll want to take over companies. Then they'll want to brainwash our children's minds. That's what Communists are like.

ANTONIO: They expect newspaper people here. From the U.S., maybe even CBS.

FULGENCIO: Who?

ANTONIO: Those are the people that do the Desi show.

FULGENCIO: How do I look?

ANTONIO: Good. Where are they?

FULGENCIO: The militia?

ANTONIO: Oscar—where is he?

FULGENCIO: Manuela is giving the crowd water, bless her.

ANTONIO: She's a good woman, my cousin.

FULGENCIO: Yes. I think Fidel is still going to get his way.

ANTONIO: Nah.

FULGENCIO: I'm just here to be counted.

Rosa and Manuela enter. Rosa is carrying paper cups. Hugo follows them with a big bottle of water that's almost empty.

MANUELA: If they want civil disobedience, we'll give them civil disobedience.

ROSA: They love you, they were so happy you gave them water.

MANUELA: Well, they're helping us.

FULGENCIO: This is all very well organized.

ROSA: But you could have sent me. But no, you went there and gave them the water yourself and thanked them. They won't forget that act of generosity!

ANTONIO: Quite a woman, my cousin.

MANUELA: Fidel isn't going to ruin transportation without me putting up a fight.

HUGO: That's telling them, Auntie.

FULGENCIO: Where's Oscar?

MANUELA: Nobody can run these buses better than us. They don't belong to anyone but us.

FULGENCIO: People always said you had the cleanest buses in this country.

ROSA: That's why they've come to protest.

HUGO: I'll go and take the bottle back to the kitchen.

MANUELA: Wait, Hugo. Do you want a glass, Antonio? Fulgencio?

ANTONIO: Gotta admit my mouth's dry.

FULGENCIO: Why not?

ROSA: Here. I'll get it.

MANUELA: Quite a crowd.

ANTONIO: I thought it'd be bigger.

ROSA: Here, Fulgencio.

MANUELA: It's big enough. He wants to see masses of organized people working towards a common goal.

ROSA: Antonio?

ANTONIO: Thanks.

MANUELA: Well, Fidel Castro. . .

ROSA: Take it to the kitchen now, Hugo.

MANUELA: I'm going to show you how it's done.

HUGO: Right. (*He exits*)

FULGENCIO: Well, we're ready.

ANTONIO: Yeah, but we need some reassurance from your husband.

FULGENCIO: We're sort of letting our necks hang out waiting for the machete.

ROSA: We got to protect our lives.

FULGENCIO: Yes, that's what I'm saying.

MANUELA: He'll be here in a minute. Go and get him, Rosa.

ANTONIO: Has he been drinking?

ROSA: What do you think?

FULGENCIO: He must be.

ANTONIO: I know I would be.

MANUELA: My husband can handle whiskey. He's watching over my mother.

ANTONIO: Jesus save her soul!

ROSA: Amen!

MANUELA: You go take over, Rosa.

ROSA: I don't get to protest?

IN THE EYE OF THE HURRICANE

MANUELA: Someone has to be with Mama.

ROSA: Yes, God save her soul!

ANTONIO: Amen.

Rosa exits.

More important to have the boss here than his maid.

FULGENCIO: That's for sure.

MANUELA: He's tense.

FULGENCIO: Of course.

ANTONIO: I know I would be also.

Mario enters.

MANUELA: How's Mama?

MARIO: The same.

ANTONIO: We're so sorry about that.

FULGENCIO: But she lived to be eighty. How many people can claim that?

MARIO: Unconscious to the fall of the bus empire.

ANTONIO: Always making a joke about everything.

MARIO: Why not?

ANTONIO: Respect your mother, at least your mother.

MARIO: Why?

ANTONIO: 'Cause of what she did for you. I respect mine and know the pain she went through to give me life. I can never, ever repay. . .

MARIO: Good. As long as you respect yours, why should you give a fuck about what I do with mine?

ANTONIO: Because I believe in a sense of decency.

MARIO: When did that start?

ANTONIO: Don't get me angry, Mario, or I'll. . .well, you won't know what hit you. I want respect for myself and my family members. . .

MARIO: What does that have to do with my mother and I?

FULGENCIO: She's his mother's cousin.

MARIO: Right.

ANTONIO: My mother thinks your mother is an angel.

MARIO: Well, she's not.

FULGENCIO: Don't upset him, he worships your family.

MARIO: Tell that to your mother.

ANTONIO: What I do today I'm doing for my fifth cousin Maria Josefa— not you, Mario—in her honor.

MARIO: I'm glad you have a reason.

ANTONIO: Want to go and fight it out?

FULGENCIO: This is not a time to fight among ourselves.

MARIO: Why not?

ANTONIO: I haven't forgotten the tricks you played on me when I was a kid!

MARIO: Good.

MANUELA: Will you two stop it!

ANTONIO: Sorry.

MARIO: Kiss my ass.

ANTONIO: Don't say those things in front of your sister.

MARIO: She knows...

MANUELA: Mario, please!

MARIO: She knows her mother said nothing when our father was shot right here. He was standing right here in this bus yard.

MANUELA: That was thirty years ago.

MARIO: Twenty-nine. I've kept an accurate account of everything—everything that's owed me.

MANUELA: Must be a big book you keep, brother.

MARIO: We never bothered to find out why he was shot, how, who shot him. We just kept the buses going for her husband.

MANUELA: For all of us.

MARIO: For you.

MANUELA: When I take a stand here today, maybe I'll pay you back a couple of pages—a couple of columns in your account book.

MARIO: No.

MANUELA: Help me! I need you to help me!

MARIO: So you two are with us, behind us!

ANTONIO: We'll lay down in front of the buses with you.

FULGENCIO: I brought my gun. (*He shows them*) Been wanting to use this baby for a long time.

MARIO: Good-looking gun.

FULGENCIO: Bought it from an ex-spy.

MARIO: American.

FULGENCIO: USA Marine.

MARIO: Impressive.

MANUELA: I don't think there should be any shooting. I think passive resistance. We lay in front of the buses. They're not going to drive over us. It wouldn't look good in the world press tomorrow. Those weird writers in France...

IN THE EYE OF THE HURRICANE

MARIO: Existentialists...

MANUELA: Yes, existentialists wouldn't like it.

FULGENCIO: Good.

ANTONIO: Strike—give them some of their own medicine.

FULGENCIO: I'll drive my car down the block, when I honk the horn three times, it means they're on their way.

MARIO: And the other bus drivers?

FULGENCIO: They refused to come with us.

ANTONIO: They said they'd drive their routes as if it were any ordinary day.

FULGENCIO: My feeling is that they'll try to confiscate these buses first and then go after the ones that are on routes.

MANUELA: As long as our protest is heard, we'll get our way.

FULGENCIO: See you soon.

MANUELA: Good.

ANTONIO: Where's cousin Oscar?

MARIO: Drinking.

MANUELA: Don't worry, he'll be here soon. He's with my mother, like I told you.

ANTONIO: I'm so sorry, Manuela, what a sad day.

MANUELA: Yes, well...

ANTONIO: She is a great woman.

MANUELA: Yes, she is.

ANTONIO: Too bad she has such an ungrateful son.

MARIO: Is that what your mother told you?

MANUELA: Leave him alone, Mario!

ANTONIO: Count on me. The other bus drivers said we were crazy to get involved, to help you. But I knew that it was my duty to help you. Is Hugo coming out?

MANUELA: Yes, of course.

ANTONIO: Good. We need all the men from the immediate family that we can get. No offence, Fulgencio.

FULGENCIO: We need more people, period.

MANUELA: More will show up.

MARIO: This won't work, sister.

MANUELA: Yes, it will. It's what we fought for—the right to protest.

MARIO: This is not a democracy anymore, sister.

MANUELA: We'll make it one again.

ANTONIO: Yes.

Antonio and Fulgencio exit.

MANUELA: Why are you so bitter, Mario? Why can't you just help me?
MARIO: I'm tired.
MANUELA: Tired of me?
MARIO: Tired of picking up the crumbs he left on the floor for me.
MANUELA: Well, if we don't do something, there won't be any crumbs left to pick.
MARIO: Whoring my future, for your husband.
MANUELA: I'm glad you didn't say "for me."
MARIO: Now risking my life, the last favor.
MANUELA: "Favor"? He did you the favor. What were you? Struggling— struggling to get Father to give you a cent, working for him, having him control you, every word you said, everything you did, so he could run around with every married woman in Guanabacoa. You were his slave.
MARIO: You didn't have to work. You stayed at home and—
MANUELA: We were all Papa's slaves—slaves to his vanity, no business sense. This family had nothing. We were going nowhere, and then Oscar—
MARIO: Made us rich.
MANUELA: Yes.
MARIO: And our father was shot, and we pretended not to notice.
MANUELA: So we could get rich. And we did. Oscar kept his promise.
MARIO: Sometimes I despise you.
MANUELA: Your own sister.
MARIO: Yes.
MANUELA: And how do you think I feel about you? You think you made me feel proud, brother?
MARIO: You always act proud. Too proud for a woman.
MANUELA: Because of Oscar, he brought me pride.

Hugo enters.

HUGO: Are they here yet?
MARIO: No.
HUGO: I'm ready for anything.
MARIO: Are you going to go galloping on your horse?
HUGO: Come on!
MANUELA: Leave him alone.

MARIO: No, you'd want to protect her, her you wouldn't want to give up. The horse is the only real love of his life.

HUGO: What's wrong with that?

MANUELA: Look, Hugo, you lay in front of number three. Mario, you in front of the six. Oscar, in front of the nine. I'll be in front of this one, the ten. Antonio, five. Fulgencio, the two.

HUGO: Yes.

MARIO: Good.

HUGO: What's good?

MARIO: We have another enemy now.

HUGO: Besides Batista.

MARIO: Besides ourselves.

MANUELA: Go and do it.

Mario and Hugo exit.

It will work. There is justice in the world. There is. I still believe in it. The number ten, bought six years ago. (*She goes to the bus*) My life.

Oscar enters with a machine gun.

OSCAR: Come on! Sons of bitches! Come on!

MANUELA: Oscar, no!

OSCAR: I'm a man! I fight like a man!

MANUELA: No, please!

OSCAR: The fight is all that matters.

MANUELA: No, what matters is not losing.

OSCAR: Come on, I'm ready for you! Sons of bitches! Reds! Assholes!

MANUELA: You're going to throw yourself in front of that bus over there, the number nine.

OSCAR: I'm going to fight! I'm going to show them that Oscar Hernandez has balls made out of steel, what fighting a man with steel balls is all about.

MANUELA: You're drunk, Oscar. This is not the time to get drunk.

OSCAR: Sometimes a drink is just the courage you need. . . . Just the fuel you need so you can function, like these buses and gasoline.

MANUELA: We're throwing ourselves in front of the buses so the world can hear us.

OSCAR: No, an eye for an eye, testicle for a testicle, dream shattered for dream shattered. Blood!

MANUELA: We're going to throw ourselves in front of the bus. I, in front of this one! You, in front of that one!

OSCAR: No, fight! *(To machine gun)* Yes, baby?

MANUELA: That's not the way.

We hear a car horn honk three times. Manuela lies in front of the bus.

Three times, that means they are on their way up the hill.

OSCAR: No, I don't like you on the ground. I don't like seeing my wife in dirt!

MANUELA: Put the machine gun inside the garage, and lie down in front of your bus.

OSCAR: The man I am is the property that I have acquired. That is Oscar Hernandez, the acreage, the boats, the tractors, the fleet of buses, the machinery and now—

MANUELA: You're going to lie on the ground and let the world know what they're doing to you. And we will be able to keep it all.

OSCAR: Without them, I'm an orphan.

Hugo enters.

A fool.

HUGO: They're here. They started on Antonio's.

MANUELA: Hide the machine gun, Oscar!

Oscar runs out.

Go to your bus, Hugo.

HUGO: I have time.

MANUELA: Don't be scared.

HUGO: All right.

MANUELA: This will work. There are working people everywhere in the world. They understand what owning something means to a person. How it makes life bearable. How it makes you have something to leave behind to your children. In the United States, that's what their society is founded on, the right to advance yourself, the right to own something, and they won't let this happen to us. They'll help us.

HUGO: They'll send in the fleet!

MANUELA: Yes!

HUGO: I'm sorry. I don't know why I believed in him, Fidel, I needed . . .

MANUELA: By tomorrow afternoon the news of our struggle to keep what belongs to us will have spread all over the world. We'll be in the *New*

York Times! And the owners of all the small businesses that keep the world from going bankrupt, that keep people from starving, will be on our side and we will win, Hugo!

HUGO *(He looks out into the street)*: They are trying to drive the first two away.

MANUELA: Fulgencio's and Antonio's?

HUGO: Mario's and mine they'll try next.

MANUELA: Go, Hugo, time to be a man.

Hugo runs out. Oscar enters. We hear the crowd cheering.

OSCAR: Fight!

MANUELA: They're all with us.

OSCAR: Of course. People love me in this town. We're going to win.

MANUELA: Fight them!

OSCAR: Yes. *(He lies down in front of the other bus)* Thank you, Manuela, for making me see.

MANUELA: Don't thank me.

OSCAR: You're so much better than me.

MANUELA: For thirty years you have been my reason.

OSCAR: Your reason?

MANUELA: My reason, for everything in life.

We hear two buses being driven away. Fumes start to come onto the stage.

(Coughing) What is that?

OSCAR: Fumes.

MANUELA: They took two of them.

OSCAR: Cowards!

MANUELA: I knew I couldn't trust them.

Antonio runs in.

ANTONIO: They had a gun to my head!

MANUELA: You should have stayed!

ANTONIO: They were going to pull the trigger.

MANUELA: No! They're not going to kill a worker.

ANTONIO: I could tell!

MANUELA: Did they?

ANTONIO: I could tell they were planning to. Who would have fed my wife and the baby? I have to think of them.

MANUELA: You let them drive the bus away.

ANTONIO: Yes, the two of them.

MANUELA: Fulgencio also?

ANTONIO: Fulgencio didn't even lay down.

MANUELA: What!

ANTONIO: He ran. They drove off before he had a chance to lay down. At least I laid down.

MANUELA: For two minutes!

ANTONIO: That's long enough to see your life running past you, and I haven't had a life yet, except for my wife and the baby.

MANUELA: I guess you're not really family.

ANTONIO: I am!

MANUELA: The family is still laying down.

ANTONIO: Manuela, respect me.

MANUELA: Why?

OSCAR: Coward!

ANTONIO: I respect, love the both of you.

MANUELA: Not enough to go down with us.

OSCAR: Smell it, smell the gasoline.

ANTONIO: I know what gasoline smells like.

OSCAR: Smell my hands, this gasoline is me, it's in my pores.

Two more buses are heard leaving the field. The fumes are now stronger. Everyone starts to cough.

ANTONIO: Well, the family just let go of two more buses.

We hear the crowd cheering.

MANUELA: Why are they cheering?

OSCAR: The crowd must be throwing things at the buses.

ANTONIO: I don't think so.

OSCAR: I know so. The people of this town look up to me. I've been good to them.

ANTONIO: People forget.

MANUELA: You and I, Oscar, we will not budge!

OSCAR: Till the newspapers get here.

MANUELA: And we'll win.

ANTONIO: Don't kill yourself for this, what's a bus? What's a business if you got yourselves, if you love...

Oscar and Manuela start to laugh.

Don't laugh at me.
MANUELA: A business becomes who you are.
OSCAR: This bus, is me.
ANTONIO: You're both losing your minds.
MANUELA: Every day your work becomes who you are.
OSCAR: Who we are.

Mario enters with two milicianos.

MARIO: Here they are, the owners.
MANUELA: Traitor!
MARIO: Why fight the future?
MANUELA: The future!
MARIO: They would have run me over.
ANTONIO: See, I told you they're intending to kill us.
MILICIANO 1: We would not...
MARIO: You got close.
MILICIANO 2: That's all.
MILICIANO 1: Testing you.
MARIO: I don't like threats.
MILICIANO 1: Now you two get up.
MANUELA: Never. Never!
OSCAR: I'm a man who listens to his wife.
MILICIANO 2: Fuck, here we go again.
MANUELA: Have other people revolted in this way?
MILICIANO 1: Only here, everybody else handed them over with dignity.
MANUELA: What do you know about dignity?
MILICIANO 2: Watch it, lady.
ANTONIO: Be careful, Manuela!
MILICIANO 1: I'm going to ask nicely once. Then we're going to take you
    off to jail. There's a mob forming outside.
MANUELA: See, what did I tell you. Good!
MILICIANO 1: All along the street. They're going quite out of control
OSCAR: That's the idea.
MILICIANO 1: We're trying to keep them from coming in and harming you.
OSCAR: Harming us. Ha!
MARIO: They're yelling, "Take them, take the buses from those imperialist
    pigs!"

MANUELA: Stop your teasing.

MILICIANO 2: If you people would just listen, maybe you'd learn something.

MILICIANO 1: Shut up, Paco! Listen.

We hear the mob yelling "Take them! Take them!"

OSCAR: I don't believe it.

MANUELA: Greedy, everybody's so greedy.

MILICIANO 1: So let's do this peacefully.

MANUELA: No.

OSCAR: I refuse!

MANUELA *(Shouting)*: We refuse you sons of bitches! Daughters of whores!

MILICIANO 1: Jesus.

MILICIANO 2: Oh God...

MILICIANO 1: Why did I get stuck with this?

MILICIANO 2: 'Cause you believe in the good of the revolution...

MILICIANO 1: Right.

MARIO: I told you, owners are owners. Hard to let go.

ANTONIO: Whose side are you on?

MARIO: My own!

MILICIANO 1: Please ma'am, sir, we've already confiscated all the others.

OSCAR: I don't believe you.

MILICIANO 1: The ones that were on their daily routes, the bus drivers just handed over.

MILICIANO 2: Willingly.

ANTONIO: At least I didn't do that.

MANUELA: Shut up, Antonio, not now!

MARIO: You will.

ANTONIO: No, I'll never drive a bus for them.

MARIO: Wait and see...

ANTONIO: Only 'cause I have to feed my family. What am I supposed to do? I don't have thousands buried anywhere...

MILICIANO 1: We got only these two buses left to confiscate.

MANUELA: Steal!

MILICIANO 1: So please, let us do it peacefully. I don't want to put two old people in jail.

OSCAR: Kill us first.

MILICIANO 1: Get in his bus.

MILICIANO 2: Yes, fine. Plan three?

MILICIANO 1: Yes, plan three.

MARIO: They're all turned against us, sister.

MANUELA: Leave us alone, Mario!

MILICIANO 1: Drive for fucking Christ sake!

ANTONIO: There's a lady here, my cousin, enough, enough!

Miliciano 2 puts the bus that Oscar is lying in front of into reverse and drives off.

OSCAR: Oh my God! We didn't think about reverse!

MARIO: Pretty smart for a bunch of morons.

MILICIANO 1: Who's a moron?

MARIO: You!

OSCAR: No, not them, us. (*He gets up, starts to walk away*)

MILICIANO 1 (*Pointing at Antonio*): Now you.

ANTONIO: Antonio. . .

MANUELA: Oscar, Oscar, where are you going?

OSCAR: To die.

MARIO: To drink.

ANTONIO: My name is Antonio, and you know 'cause I used to date your sister.

MILICIANO 1: I thought you looked familiar.

MANUELA: Don't leave me, Oscar.

OSCAR: Get up and join me.

MANUELA: Get on the other side of the bus!

MILICIANO 1: Antonio, get on the bus and drive it away.

Oscar exits.

ANTONIO: Forgive me, my dear cousin Manuela. (*He exits*)

MANUELA: How about honor, Antonio?

MARIO: Honor? When did anybody in this family have honor?

Sonia runs in.

SONIA: Mama, she's awake, the yelling in the street woke Grandma up, she's not dying, it's a miracle, a sign.

MANUELA: A trick.

MARIO: I'll tell Mama the bad news.

MANUELA: No, let her die happy, let her die successful.

MARIO: All right.

MANUELA: Don't gloat!

MILICIANO 1: Drive!

Manuela gets up and opens the hood of the bus. She lights her cigarette lighter.

MANUELA: I'm going to throw it in and blow it up!

SONIA: Mama, no! Please! No!

Miliciano 1 grabs Manuela.

MARIO: It wouldn't have worked, sister.

MILICIANO 1: Don't kick, lady!

MANUELA: Bastards!

MILICIANO 1: I was doing my job.

MANUELA: Faggot, killer, rapist!

MILICIANO 1: If you were a man, well, you wouldn't walk out alive! (*He walks away*)

MANUELA: Scum!

MILICIANO 1 (*Yelling to her*): There's a place for you here. You could have a job running the buses. We'd pay you a fair wage. If you want it, work for the people, for mankind!

MANUELA: Up yours!

We hear Antonio drive the last bus away and a crowd applauding.

Beggars, greedy beggars!

SONIA: I'm sorry, Mama, I'm . . .

MANUELA: Let them tell me to my face.

SONIA: Where are you going, Mama?

MANUELA: Hugo, stop hiding behind that tree. They're gone.

HUGO: I'm sorry.

MANUELA: Why? You acted just like the other men in this family.

HUGO: Forgive me.

MANUELA: I don't forgive them, that crowd.

HUGO: Auntie, I'll go with you . . .

MANUELA: No, Mario and I.

MARIO: Yes, sister.

MANUELA: Let's make them look at us.

HUGO: They're happy 'cause the buses belong to them now.

IN THE EYE OF THE HURRICANE

MANUELA: They resented every nickel they ever had to pay.

Mario and Manuela exit.

SONIA: Hugo, don't go.

HUGO: Let's go back in.

SONIA: I can't yet. I don't want to see Papa like that. Stay with me, Hugo.

HUGO: Yes.

SONIA: It's empty; for the first time in my life, this field is empty.

HUGO: Sonia, did you know, did you think this was going to happen?

SONIA: Yes.

HUGO: How?!

SONIA: Osvaldo heard about it a month ago. I didn't want to believe it.

HUGO: Why isn't your husband here now?

SONIA: Osvaldo thinks he has enough tragedies just dealing with his family, that I should deal with mine.

HUGO: Who would believe it!

SONIA: I believe it. I believe it now.

HUGO: I don't want to believe it.

SONIA: In my car, last night, by myself. . .I drove along the beach, speeded. . .

HUGO: How much?

SONIA: Seventy miles an hour.

HUGO: Wow, that's great for a girl!

SONIA: Yeah, it felt. . .

HUGO: Powerful.

SONIA: Why am I telling you this?

HUGO: 'Cause I'm your favorite cousin.

SONIA: You're so young.

HUGO: No, I understand about speeding. Sometimes I ride my horse at night down the beach. I'm high up. Tall. And we gallop so fast, nothing like seventy miles, but fast. Sometimes I think it's going to kill the horse, but I push her! Still a horse is not like a car, not private enough. . .I mean, the horse is there with you and she's an animal with some senses like your own, not a cold machine with no personality or mind. Indifferent. Must be something to be alone with an automobile.

SONIA: I thought I could escape.

HUGO: Escape what?

SÓNIA: My upbringing. Myself.

HUGO: Oh. . .why?

SONIA: So I could find. . .

HUGO: Excitement.

SONIA: A braver me. The other me. . .

HUGO: Two of you? I wouldn't want two of me. I've plenty to handle with one. Wait, I'll show you what Uncle Oscar taught me. (*He exits*)

SONIA: A daring me. The me that's a woman, not a child. I'm thirty years old. When does my family start? When do I become the mother? I thought when the baby was born it would happen but it didn't. Hugo? Hugo, where are you?!

Hugo runs in with the machine gun.

HUGO: This is power—speeding in a car and shooting this!

SONIA: Don't, Hugo! They'll come back and arrest us!

He pretends he's going to pull the trigger.

Please, Hugo, no!

Hugo makes the sound of a machine gun.

HUGO: See, no bullets! Couldn't find the bullets.

Manuela enters.

MANUELA: Put that away, Hugo.

HUGO: Sure. Sorry, Auntie, just having fun.

MANUELA: Pretending to be brave.

HUGO: Yes.

MANUELA: Pretense is over.

HUGO: Yes, Auntie. (*He exits*)

SONIA: What did they do?

MANUELA: They left.

SONIA: They didn't apologize?

MANUELA: They looked away. Without remorse.

SONIA: I thought you said this would work. We have nothing now, Mama.

MANUELA: I thought I knew what this country was about—what people wanted.

SONIA: You believed in the good of people. You and Papa have always been too giving.

MANUELA: Is that what your husband told you?

SONIA: Yes.

MANUELA: He's probably right.

SONIA: Seems to be.

MANUELA: You should turn to him more.

SONIA: I think I should. (*She exits*)

MANUELA (*To herself*): Oscar, you gave up.

Mario enters.

MARIO: Papa died here. We covered it up. Pretended it didn't happen so we could get somewhere. Now it's all gone.

MANUELA: I don't know how to start. I don't know how to start again. Your little girl is scared. This is all I know. (*She starts to weep*) No, I won't. (*She stops crying*)

MARIO: Good, let's go and see how Mama's doing.

MANUELA: No, I'll sit here till I can figure out a way to forgive Oscar. I hope I can. Look at it. It's empty.

She looks around. He walks to another side of the field.

MARIO: They found your body here, Papa. Someone had shot you through the back.

Blackout.

Scene 2

Lights up. Later. The dining room. Mario and Sonia are with Maria Josefa, who is in a white nightgown and sitting on a chair. Rosa is bringing in a bowl of soup for Hugo, who starts to eat it.

MARIA JOSEFA: The world was so out of reach.

MARIO: And the other side?

MARIA JOSEFA: Unreal also, like sunrise in a desert.

MARIO: What desert, Mama, you've never been in a fucking desert!

ROSA: Don't scream at her. She's weak.

HUGO: He wants to. . .

MARIO: To what?!

HUGO: Never mind!

MARIA JOSEFA: The desert of my heart, of my soul, of my longing, not tangible. Cold, I feel so goddamned cold. I don't want to start shuddering again. I don't want to shake from the cold! I hate refrigerators!

SONIA: Change of body temperature. Is that a sign, Uncle?

ROSA: Don't bury her yet!

MARIO: Who knows?

HUGO: We should call the doctor.

MARIO: What for? He told us to give her her last rites last night.

MARIA JOSEFA: I don't want the last morning of my life to be so cold. My feet are freezing, going numb.

HUGO: Frostbite.

MARIA JOSEFA: I don't know. Rub Mama's feet, Mario.

MARIO: Yes.

MARIA JOSEFA: See how you really love me.

Mario is rubbing her feet.

Girl, get me a brandy like in the old days.

ROSA: Yes, Maria Josefa, yes.

MARIA JOSEFA: And one for yourself.

ROSA: Thank you.

MARIA JOSEFA: Let me feel something in my feet.

HUGO: Where's Auntie?

SONIA: Still sitting out on the field.

HUGO: Oh.

MARIA JOSEFA: Caress my feet. It snows in Spain. My husband, your father, he knew cold up there in the mountains. He was a monument, your father, a monument to manhood. None of you came close.

ROSA: Here, you need some help.

MARIA JOSEFA: I can drink a glass of brandy on my own!

ROSA: Thank you, Lord, for answering my prayer.

MARIA JOSEFA: I've only known two real men in my life...

MARIO: Really.

MARIA JOSEFA: Your father and Oscar Hernandez, the taxicab driver, Estrella's cousin...

SONIA: Grandma, you don't mean that.

MARIA JOSEFA: I do.

IN THE EYE OF THE HURRICANE

MARIO: Well, that real man disintegrated today.

HUGO: Shut up, Uncle Mario!

MARIA JOSEFA: Oscar, never! Never!

MARIO: He let them take your beloved—

Oscar enters.

SONIA: Shut up!

OSCAR: Let him. Do it, Mario. (*He pours himself shots of whiskey, at least three, and gulps them down silently*)

MARIO: All right.

SONIA: Uncle Mario, please don't. She's dying.

MARIO: Why shouldn't she know?

SONIA: For me. Don't tell her for me, for my sake.

MARIO: Two real men. What was I?

MARIA JOSEFA: A weakling. A weakling and a pervert.

HUGO: Even she knows.

ROSA: Hugo, shut up!

MARIO: Die alone, Mama.

MARIA JOSEFA: I'm not going to die. My drink has given me energy. Death was so like life, out of reach. . .a dream, not tangible, not. . .

MARIO: Die alone. Die without my love.

SONIA: Is she dead?

Rosa goes to Maria Josefa.

ROSA: Asleep. Maybe she'll recover.

MARIO: The sugar's gone to the brain already. You heard the doctor's explanation.

ROSA: He also said she was never going to wake up!

Maria Josefa wakes up again.

MARIA JOSEFA: The only thing tangible I ever had in my life was my husband. My husband on top of me, at my breast, biting it. . .

SONIA: Grandma, please stop, please.

ROSA: She's delirious.

HUGO: Uncle Oscar, can I borrow your car?

OSCAR: They took it. They took the car also.

HUGO: Did they take yours, Sonia?!

SONIA: No. Mine is safe at my husband's house.

MARIA JOSEFA: With me, in me. I needed him so much that I began to hate him. And the hate grew to bitterness and contempt and he was killed. I thought this morning he'd walk and greet me at heaven's door, but no, he wasn't there. . . . Who are you fucking around with in heaven, husband?

HUGO: It's true. I hear Grandpa was a real stud, that somebody's husband shot him.

MARIO: All lies.

MARIA JOSEFA: What trollop has you occupied the day of my death! The day of our reunion?

OSCAR: All lost.

MARIA JOSEFA: Oscar Hernandez. Oscar, you greet me, you hold me.

Oscar goes to hold her. Maria Josefa falls asleep.

OSCAR: Tell your daughter to love me. Go outside and get her in here.

MARIO: She's asleep, Oscar, asleep. . .

HUGO: I'll go and get her. (*He runs out*)

MARIO: Come here, Oscar. Come sit by me. I'm awake.

Oscar goes and weeps in his arms.

Cry, Oscar, yes. That's good. In my arms. Yes, weep. Good. Wonderful, wonderful for me to be the person that you've turned to, that you have let the grief go with me. Yes, rest, sigh, breathe. . .

OSCAR: But. . .

MARIO: No, no buts. This moment is ours, just you and I, us, together. Me comforting you, you needing me.

OSCAR: Now Manuela knows that I am a coward.

ROSA: Sonia, can I get you some soup?

SONIA: Yes, thank you.

ROSA: Fan your grandmother.

SONIA: Yes.

Sonia fans Maria Josefa. Rosa goes into the kitchen.

MARIO: She doesn't know you. She's married to you and I thank God that you chose her, that you married my sister because that's how I became your family. But she didn't see you like I saw you. She didn't charge the passengers while you drove the bus. She wasn't at the reunions when you spoke so eloquently of the future, and the future you spoke of came to pass and everything you promised happened.

IN THE EYE OF THE HURRICANE

OSCAR: And now it's gone.

MARIO: It'll never be gone.

OSCAR: How, Mario?!

MARIO: Because you in 1935, you in 1946, you in 1954, will always be alive in my mind. "Oscar the Conqueror" is what I'll have them put on your grave.

MARIA JOSEFA (*Waking up*): Come over here, Oscar. Please be with me. Why are you crying, Oscar? Has someone died?

OSCAR: No.

MARIA JOSEFA: Are you in love with another woman?

OSCAR: Never.

MARIA JOSEFA: My daughter, does she make you truly happy?

OSCAR: Yes.

MARIA JOSEFA: Then you are crying with joy.

OSCAR: Yes. Joy that you are still alive. That I became, built, have a place in this family.

MARIA JOSEFA: I always felt safe with you, Oscar. Always so strong.

MARIO: Strong, Mama? If he's so strong, why was he crying in my arms?

SONIA: Papa. Papa, please, when is Mama going to come in? Go get her, please.

OSCAR: No.

SONIA: Please.

OSCAR: She'll come in when she understands. . .

SONIA: Understands what, Papa?

OSCAR: That we are what they want to throw away.

SONIA: No!

OSCAR: Understand that, Sonia.

SONIA: I don't want to. . .

MARIO: Oscar. I know how to save us.

OSCAR: Yes, comrades, you and I . . .

MARIA JOSEFA: And how, how did Manuela make you the happiest?

OSCAR: When she saw who she thought I was, which was so much better than the real me.

Manuela and Hugo enter.

MANUELA: That's true.

MARIO: Leave him alone.

MANUELA: I thought you like cruelty in the family.

MARIO: I love him, like a brother.

MANUELA: Liar.

MARIO: You're not a man. Trying to understand, run in a man's world, but never could.

MANUELA: Poor Mama. You're not dead.

MARIA JOSEFA: Of course not.

MANUELA: I wish you were.

MARIA JOSEFA: How dare you!

Rosa enters.

ROSA: The soup, Sonia. I heated it up.

SONIA: Thank you.

Sonia sits to eat. Manuela walks over to Maria Josefa.

MARIA JOSEFA: My recipe.

MANUELA: You haven't told her?

OSCAR: Of course not.

MANUELA: Why didn't you, Mario?

MARIO: Couldn't do that to Oscar.

MANUELA: Liar, you're capable of anything.

MARIA JOSEFA: What are you talking about?

MARIO: Usual stuff, Mama.

MANUELA: Don't be coy. You know why Oscar is so drunk, Mama? 'Cause he should have told you.... Our buses—

MARIA JOSEFA: Told me you make him happy. Aren't you the lucky one?

SONIA: I'm leaving.

HUGO: Take me with you.

SONIA: All right.

HUGO: We'll go for a ride, take it up to eighty.

SONIA: Good. If Osvaldo comes by here, tell him Hugo and I went racing.

MARIA JOSEFA: She shouldn't race without her husband!

ROSA: Yes, I'll tell him. Be careful.

They exit.

OSCAR: Cruel wife.... You've turned cruel.

MARIO: Oscar, pour yourself a drink and one for me and let's toast to the past, to our past, glorious.... Enough stories to tell to fill up the rest of your life.

OSCAR: I don't want the old lady to die unhappy.

IN THE EYE OF THE HURRICANE

MARIO: She won't believe her.

MANUELA: Mama, God wanted you to stay alive so I could tell you one last thing, so you could learn an important lesson before you leave this earth. In the end, all the years of struggle, the greed, the need, the work, the constant preoccupation with profit, future product—

OSCAR: Success, goddamnit! All we wanted was to be successful.

ROSA: Can I get anybody anything?

MANUELA: In the end...

MARIO: Have a break for the rest of your life.

ROSA: No, I like it here.

MANUELA: In the end, Mama, it wasn't worth it. They're gone, our buses are gone. The new government confiscated them. They own them now. They're no longer ours. We no longer own a business, Mama!

MARIA JOSEFA: What did I tell you about men with beards?! What did I tell you?!

MANUELA: No more business, no more country, no more profits.

MARIA JOSEFA: And you did nothing.

MANUELA: I threw myself in front of the bus.

ROSA: Good for you.

MARIO: But it didn't work.

MARIA JOSEFA: Go and get them back, Oscar.

OSCAR: I can't. He's crippled me. Fidel won. There's nothing I can do. I can't move. I'm frozen here.

MARIA JOSEFA: Rosa!

ROSA: What do you want, ma'am?

MARIA JOSEFA: To go to my room to die.

ROSA: Yes, ma'am.

They start to exit.

Aren't any of you coming?

MARIA JOSEFA: I want Mario.

MARIO: Only if you tell me that I am as much of a man as anybody else.

MARIA JOSEFA: Unfortunately, son, you are.

MARIO: And you love me.

MARIA JOSEFA: All mothers love their children.

OSCAR: I have to vomit, the drinks, I have to...

MARIO: In a moment. I'll go in, in a moment.

Maria Josefa gestures that that is fine as Rosa helps her to her bedroom.

OSCAR: I gotta run...I gotta vomit.

MANUELA: If you have to vomit, vomit on my lap but stay here with me. Go on, Mario. Do it. Betray him now.

MARIO: Papa died. Was it an accident? A political move? Did you order it? Who will ever know. But I do know that you used it to take control of the business. To take it away from the family so you could have it for yourselves. That's all I'm doing using this opportunity for myself. It's fair. It's fair after all these years.

OSCAR: What are you talking about?

MANUELA: They offered him a job.

OSCAR: Who?

MANUELA: Fidel...

OSCAR: Who told you?

MANUELA: Antonio, when he came to pick up his tool box, he told me that everybody had to make a living...et cetera, et cetera, et cetera...and with his last et cetera he told me what a traitor you've turned into, brother. Now Fidel is your savior. He's going to let you pretend to be my husband. Was he lying, Mario?

MARIO: No. Not Fidel, exactly, no. One of his men offered me the job. But...

OSCAR: You said no, of course, good boy. You've always been a good boy.

MARIO: Manager. Managing the buses. Regular income.

OSCAR: Bastards thinking you'd betrayed me. Filthy bastards.

MANUELA: He has betrayed you.

OSCAR: No, the family sticks together. You always underestimated your brother.

MANUELA: You're taking the job.

MARIO: Yes. I am.

Oscar pushes Manuela aside and grabs Mario by his shirt collar. Manuela sits down and lights a cigarette.

OSCAR: Justice is on my side! Justice! You fucking queer! Bastard!

Oscar starts to hit Mario. Mario begins to shake.

MARIO: I'll have them arrest you. They're coming in...in a few minutes. I'm giving them the books, so they know how much money we make.

Sonia enters. She is hysterical.

IN THE EYE OF THE HURRICANE

SONIA: Mama! My car! They came for it! Osvaldo was going to hand it over to them 'cause it was in your name. Because it wasn't really mine.

MANUELA: Forget about it.

OSCAR: I'm gonna kill you. Right out there. Two shots and you're taken care of.

MARIO: Like my father?

OSCAR: Shut up!

SONIA *(To Manuela)*: And Hugo said the time to fight is now! And he got in the car, the milicianos started shooting at him, and Hugo smashed my car against the wall.

MANUELA: Is he all right? Have they shot him...oh God...

MARIO: That boy would pick the wrong time to be heroic.

SONIA: They arrested him.

MARIO: Let him spend the night in jail, it'll do him good.

SONIA: Osvaldo is trying to get Hugo out of jail. He's really angry at me. I always get into marital problems because of my family. Mama, I thought it was my car, but it wasn't. Why isn't anything mine?

MANUELA: 'Cause you haven't earned it.

During this, Oscar has been looking for a gun. He finds one. He begins to load it.

OSCAR: Osvaldo should learn how to use a gun.

SONIA: Jesus, Jesus! You're all as crazy as Hugo...Jesus!

OSCAR: Manuela! Sonia! Under the table!

Sonia and Manuela drop to the ground and start to crawl under the table.

I want you.

MARIO: Drop the gun. There is such a thing as law! Don't you fear the law?

OSCAR: A bullet. That's the law in this country.... Always been... *(He aims but can't shoot)* ...My hands are shaking...

MARIO: Too much booze. Don't lose all of your dignity, please, Oscar. You had so much dignity...I loved and hated you so...I can tell you now. I loved and hated you more than anything, more than my own life. Do you understand?...You must have known.... Do you know what it's been like to live just outside, so near but at the same time so apart...

OSCAR: Apart from what?

MARIO: Business, the family, business.

Oscar shoots in the air. Sonia screams. Manuela gets up. Rosa enters.

ROSA: She's asleep. Don't wake her up. I want her to die in her sleep like she deserves.

MANUELA: You scared the hell out of Sonia. Oscar, hand me the gun.

Oscar hands her the gun.

Mario, you betrayed a man whose only crime was wanting to help you.

OSCAR: I'm going to Fidel. I'm going to tell him exactly what I think of him. What a liar he's been. That all he is, is a liar.

MANUELA: I'm going with you.

MARIO: They'll arrest both of you.

OSCAR: They've already killed me. They can't do anything else.

MANUELA: Take me with you.

OSCAR: Of course.

MANUELA: Through it all, together. He and I, Mario, together. Married. Blood really mixing with blood. Look at Sonia. That's Oscar and I, blessed by God.

MARIO: Fidel is the first chance I've ever had to be the boss.

ROSA: Working for Fidel, not boss. Like when Manuela let me decide what pot I wanted to buy for the rice. I got to pick it. Still, it didn't belong to me.

MARIO: We all own everything now. All equals.

SONIA: I'm sitting in the room with Grandma. I'm gonna pray for all of us. Prayer in moments like this is the only salvation. Put it all in Jesus' hands. Right, Rosa?

ROSA: Right, don't let her wake up. . .

SONIA: Thank you, Rosa. (*She goes to the bedroom*)

MANUELA: Because I was a woman, I was supposed to be weak? You hated me because I developed a mind. 'Cause I had a business sense. I could seduce Oscar and run our empire.

OSCAR: Let's go.

MANUELA: Here, Rosa. Bury this somewhere. (*She hands Rosa the gun*)

ROSA: Be careful. Please, be careful.

MARIO: What good is your business sense going to do you in jail?

MANUELA: I'll plan our revenge. It isn't over yet, Mario. Not yet.

OSCAR: Not ever.

They exit.

MARIO: I need a drink. Pour me a drink, Rosa.

ROSA: Yes, sir.

MARIO: They'll want the books. Where are they kept?

ROSA: In here. (*She points to the sideboard*)

MARIO: I don't have the key. (*He takes Oscar's gun from Rosa's hands and shoots the lock off the sideboard*)

ROSA: You work fast.

MARIO: When you're changing the world, speed is your friend. (*He takes the ledgers and begins to look through them*) So much money. They stole so much goddamned money! Mafiosos!

ROSA: May God have pity on you, Mario.

MARIO: I've fallen from grace? Branded forever. Isn't that right, Rosa?

ROSA: Yes.

MARIO: In jail. . . . When they're in jail, they'll begin to know what life in this house was like for me.

ROSA: This house is too beautiful to be a jail.

MARIO: When you sleep in a single bed against the wall and on the other side of the wall your mother sleeps, and it's been going on like this for more than fifty years, it is a jail.

ROSA: You should have moved the bed.

MARIO: Get me a brandy.

Rosa pours a brandy and hands it to Mario. The lights fade to black.

END OF PLAY

BROKEN EGGS

For Jamie and Dena

*And to Harriett, Gilda
and their daughters*

CHARACTERS

SONIA MARQUEZ HERNANDEZ, a Cuban woman
LIZETTE, Sonia's daughter, nineteen years old
MIMI, Sonia's daughter
OSCAR, Sonia's son
MANUELA RIPOLL, Sonia's mother
OSVALDO MARQUEZ, Sonia's ex-husband
MIRIAM MARQUEZ, Osvaldo's sister
ALFREDO MARQUEZ, Osvaldo's and Miriam's father

TIME

A hot January day, 1979.

PLACE

A country club in Woodland Hills, California, a suburb of Los Angeles.

BROKEN EGGS

ACT ONE

A waiting room off the main ballroom of a country club in Woodland Hills, California, a suburb of Los Angeles. The room is decorated for a wedding. Up center, sliding glass doors leading to the outside; stage right, a hallway leading to the dressing room; stage left, an archway containing the main entrance to the room and a hallway leading to the ballroom. A telephone booth in one corner. Two round tables, one set with coffee service and the other for the cake.

In the dark, we hear Mimi whistling the wedding march. As the lights come up, Lizette is practicing walking down the aisle. Mimi is drinking a Tab and watching Lizette. They are both dressed in casual clothes.

MIMI: I never thought that any of us would get married, after all—

LIZETTE: Pretend you come from a happy home.

MIMI: We were the audience to one of the worst in the history of the arrangement.

LIZETTE: Well, I'm going to pretend that Mom and Dad are together for today.

MIMI: That's going to be hard to do if that mustached bitch, whore, cunt, Argentinian Nazi shows up to your wedding.

LIZETTE: Daddy promised me that his new wife had no wish to be here. She's not going to interfere.

Mimi starts to gag.

Mimi, why are you doing this.

MIMI: The whole family is going to be here.

LIZETTE: They're our family. Don't vomit again, Mimi, my wedding.

MANUELA (*Offstage*): Why didn't the bakery deliver it?

MIMI: Oh, no!

LIZETTE: Oh my God.

THE FLOATING ISLAND PLAYS

Mimi and Lizette run to the offstage dressing room.

MANUELA *(Offstage):* Who ever heard of getting up at 6 A.M.?

SONIA *(Offstage):* Mama, please—

Manuela and Sonia enter. Sonia is carrying two large cake boxes. Manuela carries a third cake box.

MANUELA: Well, why didn't they?

SONIA: Because the Cuban bakery only delivers in downtown L.A. They don't come out this far.

Manuela and Sonia start to assemble the cake.

MANUELA: Then Osvaldo should have picked it up.

SONIA: It was my idea.

MANUELA: He should still pick it up, he's the man.

SONIA: He wanted to get a cake from this place, with frosting on it. But I wanted a cake to be covered with meringue, like mine.

MANUELA: You let your husband get away with everything.

SONIA: I didn't let him have a mistress.

MANUELA: Silly girl, she ended up being his wife!

SONIA: That won't last forever.

MANUELA: You were better off with a mistress. Now you're the mistress.

SONIA: Please, help me set up the cake. . . . Osvaldo thought we should serve the cake on paper plates. I said no. There's nothing worse than paper plates. They only charge a dime a plate for the real ones and twenty dollars for the person who cuts it. I never saw a paper plate till I came to the USA.

MANUELA: She used witchcraft to take your husband away, and you did nothing.

SONIA: I will.

MANUELA: Then put powder in his drinks, like the witch lady told you to do.

SONIA: I won't need magic to get him back, Mama, don't put powders in his drink. It'll give him indigestion.

MANUELA: Don't worry.

SONIA: Swear to me. On my father's grave.

The cake is now assembled.

MANUELA: I swear by the Virgin Mary, Saint Teresa my patron saint and

BROKEN EGGS

all the saints, that I will not put anything into your husband's food . . . as long as his slut does not show up. Here. *(She hands Sonia a little bottle)*

SONIA: No.

MANUELA: In case you need it.

SONIA: I won't.

MANUELA: You might want it later. It also gives you diarrhea for at least three months. For love, you kiss the bottle, and thank the Virgin Mary. For diarrhea, you do the sign of the cross twice.

SONIA: All right.

MANUELA: If your father was alive, he'd shoot him for you.

SONIA: That's true.

MANUELA: Help me roll the cake out.

SONIA: No. They'll do it. They're getting the room ready now. They don't want us in there. We wait here—the groom's family across the way.

MANUELA: The Jews?

SONIA: The Rifkins. Then we make our entrance.

MANUELA: I see.

SONIA *(Looks at cake)*: Perfect. Sugary and white . . . pure.

MANUELA: Beautiful.

SONIA: I'm getting nervous.

MANUELA: It's your daughter's wedding. A very big day in a mother's life, believe me.

SONIA: Yes, a wedding is a big day.

MANUELA: The day you got married your father told me, "We are too far away from our little girl." I said to him, "But, Oscar, we live only a mile away." He said, "You know that empty acre on the street where she lives now?" I said "Yes." He said, "I bought it and we are building another house there, then we can still be near our little girl."

SONIA: He loved me.

MANUELA: Worshipped you.

SONIA: I worshipped him. He'll be proud.

MANUELA: Where's your ex-husband, he's late.

Lizette enters and makes herself a cup of coffee. Sonia helps her.

SONIA: So how do you feel, Lizette, my big girl?

LIZETTE: I'm shaking.

MANUELA: That's good. You should be scared.

LIZETTE: Why, Grandma?

MANUELA: You look dark, did you sit out in the sun again?

LIZETTE: Yes, I wanted to get a tan.

MANUELA: Men don't like that, Lizette.

LIZETTE: How do you know?

SONIA: Mama, people like tans in America.

MANUELA: Men like women with white skin.

LIZETTE: That's a lie. They don't.

MANUELA: Don't talk back to me like that.

SONIA: No fights today, please, no fights. Lizette, tell her you're sorry. I'm nervous. I don't want to get a migraine, I want to enjoy today.

LIZETTE: Give me a kiss, Grandma.

They kiss.

Everything looks so good.

SONIA: It should—eight thousand dollars.

MANUELA: We spent more on your wedding and that was twenty-nine years ago. He should spend money on his daughter.

SONIA: He tries. He's just weak.

MANUELA: Don't defend him.

SONIA: I'm not.

MANUELA: Hate him. Curse him.

SONIA: I love him.

MANUELA: Sonia! Control yourself.

LIZETTE: He's probably scared to see everybody.

MANUELA: Good, the bastard.

Lizette exits to dressing room.

SONIA: Did I do a good job? Are you pleased by how it looks? *(She looks at the corsages and boutonnieres on a table)* Purples, pinks and white ribbons . . . tulle. Mama, Alfredo, Pedro. . . . No, not Pedro's . . . Oscar's. . . . He just looks like Pedro. Pedro! He got lost. He lost himself and then we lost him.

MANUELA: Sonia!

SONIA: I'll pin yours on, Mama.

MANUELA: Later, it'll wilt if you pin it now.

Miriam enters. She is wearing a beige suit and a string of pearls.

BROKEN EGGS

SONIA: Miriam, you're here on time. Thank you, Miriam.

MIRIAM: Sonia, look. *(Points at pearls)* They don't match. That means expensive. I bought them for the wedding.

MANUELA: Miriam, how pretty you look!

MIRIAM: Do you think the Jews will approve?

MANUELA: They're very nice, the Rifkins. They don't act Jewish. Lizette told me they put up a Christmas tree but what for I said to her?

MIRIAM: To fit in?

MANUELA: Why? Have you seen your brother?

MIRIAM: He picked us up last night from the airport.

MANUELA: Did he say anything to you?

MIRIAM: Yes, how old he's getting. . . . That's all he talks about.

MANUELA: Where's your husband?

MIRIAM: He couldn't come: business.

MANUELA: That's a mistake.

MIRIAM: I'm glad I got away.

MANUELA: But is he glad to be rid of you?

SONIA: Mama, go and see if Lizette needs help, please.

MANUELA: All right. Keep your husband happy, that's the lesson to learn from all this. Keep them happy. Let them have whatever they want. . . . Look at Sonia. *(She exits to dressing room)*

SONIA: Thank God for a moment of silence. Osvaldo this, Osvaldo that. Powder. Curse him. Poisons, shit . . .

MIRIAM: Are you all right? That faggot brother of mine is not worth one more tear: coward, mongoloid, retarded creep.

SONIA: Does he look happy to you?

MIRIAM: No.

SONIA: He looks sad?

MIRIAM: He always looked sad. Now he looks old and sad.

SONIA: Fear?

MIRIAM: Doesn't the Argentinian make him feel brave?

SONIA: He'll be mine again. He'll remember what it was like before the revolution. Alfredo and you being here will remind him of that. He'll remember our wedding—how perfect it was; how everything was right . . . the party, the limo, walking through the rose garden late at night, sleeping in the terrace room. I'm so hot I feel like I have a fever.

MIRIAM: "My darling children, do not go near the water, the sharks will eat you up." That's the lesson we were taught.

SONIA: Today I am going to show Osvaldo who's in control. Be nice to him today.

MIRIAM: He left you three months after your father died. He went because he knew you had no defense. He went off with that twenty-nine-year-old wetback. You know, we *had* to come here, but they *want* to come here. And you still want him back?

SONIA: If he apologizes, yes.

MIRIAM: Don't hold your breath. He lets everyone go. Pedro needed him—

SONIA: Don't accuse him of that, he just forgot.

MIRIAM: What? How could he forget. Pedro was our brother.

SONIA: He got so busy here working, that he forgot, he couldn't help him anyway. He was here, Pedro stayed in Cuba, you were in Miami, and I don't think anyone should blame anyone about that. No one was to blame!

MIRIAM: Oh, I'm having an attack . . . *(She shows Sonia her hands)* See how I'm shaking? It's like having a seizure. Where's water?

Sonia gets her a glass of water. She takes two valium.

You take one, too.

SONIA: No. Thank you.

Mimi enters, goes to the pay phone, dials.

MIRIAM: A valium makes you feel like you are floating in a warm beach.

SONIA: Varadero?

MIRIAM: Varadero, the Gulf of Mexico, Santa María del Mar. It's because of these little pieces of magic that I escaped from the path. I did not follow the steps of my brothers and end up an alcoholic.

SONIA: Osvaldo never drank a lot.

MIRIAM: You forget.

SONIA: Well, drinking was not the problem.

MANUELA *(Entering)*: I made Mimi call the brothel to see why your husband's late.

MIRIAM: Where's Lizette?

MANUELA: Down the hall. It says "Dressing Room."

MIRIAM: I got five hundred dollars, brand-new bills. *(She exits)*

SONIA: The world I grew up in is out of style; will we see it again, Mama?

MIMI *(Comes out of the phone booth)*: She answered. She said "Yes?" I said "Where's my father?" She said "Gone." I said "Already!" She said "I'm getting ready for . . . ." I said "For what? Your funeral?" She hung up on me. She sounded stoned.

MANUELA: Sonia, someday it will be reality again, I promise.

MIMI: What?

SONIA: Cuba. Cuba will be a reality.

MIMI: It was and is a myth. Your life there is mythical.

MANUELA: That's not true. Her life was perfect. In the mornings, after she was married, Oscar would get up at six-thirty and send one of his bus drivers ten miles to buy bread from her favorite bakery, to buy bread for his little married girl.

SONIA: At around nine, I would wake up and walk out the door through the yard to the edge of the rose garden and call, "Papa, my bread."

MANUELA: The maid would run over, cross the street and hand her two pieces of hot buttered bread . . .

SONIA: I'd stick my hand through the gate and she'd hand me the bread. I'd walk back—into my mother-in-law's kitchen, and my coffee and milk would be waiting for me.

MIMI: Did you read the paper?

SONIA: The papers? I don't think so.

MIMI: Did you think about the world?

SONIA: No. I'd just watch your father sleep and eat my breakfast.

MANUELA: Every morning, "Papa, my bread." *(She goes to the outside doors and stays there, staring out)*

MIMI: You will never see it again. Even if you do go back, you will seem out of place; it will never be the same.

SONIA: No? You never saw it.

MIMI: And I will never see it.

SONIA: Never say never!

MIMI: What do you mean "Never say never"?!

SONIA: Never say never. Never is not real. It is a meaningless word. Always is a word that means something. Everything will happen always. The things that you feared and made your hands shake with horror, and you thought "not to me," will happen always.

MIMI: Stop it!

SONIA: I have thoughts, ideas. Just because I don't speak English well doesn't mean that I don't have feelings. A voice—a voice that thinks, a mind that talks.

MIMI: I didn't say that.

SONIA: So never say never, dear. Be ready for anything. Don't die being afraid. Don't, my darling.

MIMI: So simple.

Miriam enters.

SONIA: Yes, very simple, darling.

MIRIAM: What was simple?

SONIA: Life, when we were young.

MIRIAM: A little embarrassing, a little dishonest, but without real care; that's true. A few weeks ago I read an ad. It said "Liberate Cuba through the power of Voodoo." There was a picture of Fidel's head with three pins stuck through his temples.

MANUELA: They should stick pins in his penis.

SONIA: Mama! *(She laughs)*

MANUELA: Bastard.

MIRIAM: The idea was that if thousands of people bought the product, there would be a great curse that would surely kill him—all that for only $11.99. Twelve dollars would be all that was needed to overthrow the curse of our past.

Lizette enters wearing a robe.

MANUELA: We should try everything, anything.

LIZETTE: Today is my wedding, it is really happening in an hour, here, in Woodland Hills, California, Los Angeles. The United States of America, 1979. No Cuba today please, no Cuba today.

SONIA: Sorry.

MIMI: You want all the attention.

SONIA: Your wedding is going to be perfect. We are going to win this time.

LIZETTE: Win what?

MANUELA: The battle.

MIRIAM: "Honest woman" versus the "whore."

MIMI: But who's the "honest woman" and who's the "whore"?

MANUELA: Whores can be easily identified—they steal husbands.

MIRIAM: They're from Argentina.

SONIA: They say "yes" to everything. The good ones say "no."

LIZETTE: And we're the good ones.

SONIA: Yes. I am happy today. You are the bride, the wedding decorations came out perfect and we are having a party. Oo, oo, oo, oo, oo . . . *uh.*

The women all start doing the conga in a circle. They sing. Osvaldo enters.

Join the line.
LIZETTE: In back of me, Daddy.
MIRIAM: In front of me, Osvaldo.

They dance. Miriam gooses Osvaldo.

OSVALDO: First I kiss my daughter— *(He kisses Lizette)* then my other little girl— *(He kisses Mimi)* then my sister—

He and Miriam blow each other a kiss.

—then my wife. *(He kisses Sonia)*
SONIA: Your ex-wife.
OSVALDO: My daughter's mother.
SONIA: That's right.

Miriam lights a cigarette and goes outside.

MIMI: We were together once, family: my mom, my dad, my big sister, my big brother. We ate breakfast and dinner together and drove down to Florida on our vacations, looked at pictures of Cuba together.
SONIA: And laughed, right?
MIMI: And then Papa gave us up.
OSVALDO: I never gave you up.
MIMI: To satisfy his urge.
MANUELA: Stop right now.
OSVALDO: Don't ever talk like that again.
SONIA: Isn't it true?
OSVALDO: It's more complex than that.
SONIA: More complex—how? No, stop.
LIZETTE: Please stop.
MANUELA: Don't fight.
MIMI: You see, Daddy, I understand you.
OSVALDO: You don't.
MIMI: I try.
OSVALDO: So do I.
MIMI: You don't.
OSVALDO: I'm going outside.

LIZETTE: Come, sit with me.

SONIA: You have to start getting dressed.

LIZETTE: Thank you for making *me* happy.

OSVALDO: I try.

Lizette and Osvaldo exit to dressing room.

SONIA: Mimi, no more today. Please, no more.

MIMI: When you're born the third child, the marriage is already half apart, and being born into a family that's half over, half apart, is a disturbing thing to live with.

SONIA: Where did you read that?

MIMI: I didn't read it. It's my opinion. Based on my experience, of my life.

SONIA: We were never half apart.

MIMI: No, but that's what it felt like.

MANUELA: It's unheard of. It's unbelievable—

MIMI: What is she talking about now?

MANUELA: A Catholic does not get a divorce. They have a mistress and a wife but no divorce, a man does not leave everything.

SONIA *(To Mimi)*: As difficult as it might be for you to understand, we were together, and a family when you were born. I wanted, we wanted, to have you. We had just gotten to the U.S., Lizette was ten months old. Your father had gotten his job as an accountant. We lived behind a hamburger stand between two furniture stores, away from everything we knew, afraid of everything around us. We were alone, no one spoke Spanish. Half of the people thought we were Communist, the other half traitors to a great cause; three thousand miles away from our real lives. But I wanted you and we believed in each other more than ever before. We were all we had.

MIMI: I wish it would have always stayed like that.

SONIA: So do I.

MANUELA: In Cuba, not in California, we want our Cuba back.

MIMI: It's too late for that, Grandma.

MANUELA: No.

MIMI: They like their government.

MANUELA: Who?

MIMI: The people who live there like socialism.

MANUELA: No. Who told you that?

MIMI: He's still in power, isn't he?

BROKEN EGGS

MANUELA: Because he oppresses them. He has the guns, Fidel has the bullets. Not the people. He runs the concentration camps. He has Russia behind him. China. We have nothing behind us. My cousins are starving there.

MIMI: At least they know who they are.

MANUELA: You don't? Well, I'll tell you. You're Manuela Sonia Marquez Hernandez. A Cuban girl. Don't forget what I just told you.

MIMI: No, Grandma. I'm Manuela Sonia Marquez, better known as Mimi Mar-kwez. I was born in Canoga Park. I'm a first-generation white Hispanic American.

MANUELA: No you're not. You're a Cuban girl. Memorize what I just told you.

Lizette and Osvaldo enter. Lizette is in her bra and slip.

LIZETTE: My dress, Mama, help me, time to dress.

SONIA: The bride is finally ready, Mama, help me dress her in her wedding dress. Miriam, Mimi, she's going to put on her wedding dress.

Miriam enters.

MANUELA: You're going to look beautiful.

SONIA: And happy, right, dear?

LIZETTE: I'm happy. This is a happy day, like they tell you in church, your baptism, your first communion and your wedding. Come on, Mimi.

All the women except Sonia exit to the dressing room.

SONIA: That's how I felt. I felt just like her.

OSVALDO: When, Sonia?

SONIA: Twenty-nine years ago.

Sonia exits to the dressing room. Osvaldo goes to the bar and pours himself a double of J&B. Alfredo enters.

ALFREDO: You the guard?

OSVALDO: No.

ALFREDO: Drinking so early in the morning.

OSVALDO: My nerves, Daddy.

ALFREDO: Nervous, you made your bed, lie in it.

OSVALDO: I do. I do lie in it.

ALFREDO: So don't complain.

OSVALDO: I'm just nervous, little Lizette is a woman now.

ALFREDO: You're lucky.

OSVALDO: Why?

ALFREDO: She turned out to be decent.

OSVALDO: Why wouldn't she?

ALFREDO: In America it's hard to keep girls decent, especially after what you did.

OSVALDO: I never deserted them.

ALFREDO: But divorce, you're an idiot. Why get married twice, once is enough. You can always have one on the side and keep your wife. But to marry your mistress is stupid, crazy and foolish. It's not done, son. It's not decent.

OSVALDO: And you know a lot about decency?!

ALFREDO: I stayed married.

OSVALDO: Daddy, she loved me. I loved her. We couldn't be away from each other. She left her husband.

ALFREDO: She wanted your money.

OSVALDO: What money?

ALFREDO: To a little immigrant you're Rockefeller.

OSVALDO: Women only wanted you for your money.

ALFREDO: I know. And I knew how to use my position.

OSVALDO: She loves me.

ALFREDO: Good, she loves you—you should have taken her out dancing. Not married her.

OSVALDO: I did what I wanted to do, that's all.

ALFREDO: You did what your mistress wanted you to do. That is all.

OSVALDO: I wanted to marry her. That's why I did it. I just didn't do what my family thought I was supposed to do.

ALFREDO: You're still a silly boy. (Looking at wedding decorations and cake) Well, very nice. Sonia still has taste.

OSVALDO: Yes, she does.

ALFREDO: When she was young I was always impressed by the way she dressed, by the way she looked, how she spoke. The way she treated my servants, my guests.

OSVALDO: She was very well brought up.

ALFREDO: Now your new one is common, right?

OSVALDO: She loves me. Respect her, please.

ALFREDO: So did Sonia. The only thing the new one had to offer is that she groans a little louder and played with your thing a little longer, right?

OSVALDO: That's not true.

ALFREDO: Boring you after five years?

OSVALDO: . . . A little.

ALFREDO: Then why?

Lizette enters. She is dressed in her bride's dress.

LIZETTE: I'm ready for my photographs, Bride and Father.

OSVALDO: You look better than Elizabeth Taylor in *Father of the Bride.*

ALFREDO: Sweetheart, you look beautiful.

LIZETTE: Thank you. He took pictures of Mama dressing me, putting on my veil. Now he wants pictures of you and me—than Mama, you and me—then Grandpa, you and me and Miriam—then Mama and me and Grandma—then with Mimi, et cetera, et cetera, et cetera, et cetera; all the combinations that make up my family.

OSVALDO: Are you excited?

LIZETTE: Yes, I am. And nervous, Daddy, I'm so excited and nervous.

SONIA *(Enters)*: Time for the pictures, Mimi will call me when he needs me again.

OSVALDO: Do I look handsome?

ALFREDO: Look at this place, beautiful, Sonia, a beautiful job. *(He gives Sonia a little kiss)*

SONIA: Thank you.

ALFREDO: She knows how to throw parties. Hmmm, Osvaldo, with taste. With class.

OSVALDO: With class.

SONIA: Osvaldo, come here a moment. Pin my corsage.

Osvaldo goes over to the table with the corsages on it.

I bought myself a purple orchid. It goes with the dress. I bought your wife the one with the two white gardenias. I figured she'd be wearing white, trying to compete with the bride. She's so young and pure, hmmm . . . *(She laughs)*

OSVALDO: She's not coming.

SONIA: It was a joke; I was making a little joke. I can joke about it now. Laugh. Did you dream about me again last night?

OSVALDO: Shh. Not in front of Lizette.

SONIA: I want to.

OSVALDO: We spent too much money on this, don't you think?

SONIA: No, I don't. I could have used more. Mama said they spent twice as much on our wedding.

OSVALDO: Did you tell them the exact number of people that RSVP'd so that we don't have to pay money for extra food?

SONIA: Lizette did, I can't communicate with them, my English—

OSVALDO: Your English is fine. I don't want to spend extra money.

SONIA: How much did you spend on your last wedding?

OSVALDO: She paid for it, she saved her money. She works, you know. She wanted a fancy wedding. I already had one. A sixteen-thousand-dollar one, according to your mother.

SONIA: Didn't *she*? Or was she not married to the guy she left for you?

OSVALDO: She was married. She doesn't live with people.

SONIA: Fool. When you got near fifty you turned into a fool; a silly, stupid, idiotic fool.

LIZETTE: No fights today.

Osvaldo and Lizette start to exit.

SONIA: I'm sorry. I swear, no fights . . . Osvaldo . . .

OSVALDO: Yes?

SONIA: You look debonair.

OSVALDO: Thank you, Sonia.

ALFREDO: Don't let it go to your head.

OSVALDO: You look magnifique.

SONIA: Thank you, Osvaldo.

Lizette and Osvaldo exit to the ballroom.

ALFREDO: Don't let it go to your head.

SONIA: He's insecure, about his looks.

ALFREDO: I tried to talk some sense into my son.

SONIA: Today we'll be dancing every dance together, in front of everybody. And I'll be the wife again. Divorces don't really count for Catholics. We're family, him and me.

ALFREDO: When you married him and moved in with us, I always thought you were like brother and sister.

SONIA: No, lovers. Stop teasing me. He's my only friend.

ALFREDO: Even now?

BROKEN EGGS

SONIA: Always, Alfredo, forever.

MIRIAM (*Enters from the ballroom*): Sonia, your turn for more snapshots—Father, Mother and Bride.

SONIA: She's happy, don't you think?

MIRIAM: The bride is in heaven.

SONIA: Excuse me, Alfredo, if you want breakfast, ask the waiter.

Sonia exits. Miriam sits down. Alfredo looks at the coffee and sits down.

ALFREDO: Go get me a cup of coffee.

MIRIAM: No. Call the waiter, he'll get it for you.

ALFREDO: You do it for me.

MIRIAM: No.

ALFREDO: When did you stop talking to waiters?

MIRIAM: When I started talking to the gardener.

ALFREDO: What a sense of humor! What wit! What a girl, my daughter.

MIRIAM: Ruthless, like her dad.

ALFREDO: Exactly like me; you need to conquer. Go! Make sure it's hot!

Miriam pours the coffee.

If I were your husband I'd punish you every night: no money for you, no vacations, no cars, no credit cards, no pills, no maid. The way you exhibit yourself in your "see-through blouses" with no bras, and your skimpy bikinis.

MIRIAM (*Teasing Alfredo*): Ooooh!

ALFREDO: How many horns did you put on his head?

MIRIAM: It excites him.

ALFREDO: That's not true.

MIRIAM: He feels lucky when he gets me, that I did not wither like all the other girls from my class, from our country, with their backward ways. Sugar, Daddy?

ALFREDO: Two lumps. No, three, and plenty of milk.

MIRIAM: There's only cream.

ALFREDO: Yes, cream is fine.

MIRIAM: Here, Daddy.

ALFREDO (*Takes one sip and puts coffee down*): What a vile taste American coffee has.

MIRIAM: I'm used to it, less caffeine.

ALFREDO: You did keep in shape.

Mimi enters from the ballroom in her bridesmaid's gown.

MIRIAM: So did you. Greed and lust keep us in shape.

MIMI: Grandpa, your turn. Both sets of grandparents, the Cubans and the Jews, the bride and the groom.

ALFREDO: How do I look, sweetheart?

MIMI: Dandy, Grandpa, dandy.

Alfredo exits.

Who do you lust after?

MIRIAM: Your father.

MIMI: Your own brother?!

MIRIAM: I was joking—your father's too old now. Your brother, maybe.

MIMI: You are wild.

MIRIAM: If I would have been born in this country, to be a young girl in this country, without eyes staring at you all the time. To have freedom. I would never have gotten married. I wanted to be a tightrope walker in the circus . . . that's what I would have wanted.

MIMI: I never feel free.

MIRIAM: Do you get to go to a dance alone?

MIMI: Naturally.

MIRIAM: Then you have more freedom than I ever did.

MIMI: How awful for you.

MIRIAM: It made you choke, you felt strangled.

MIMI: What did you do?

MIRIAM: I found revenge.

MIMI: How?

MIRIAM: I'll tell you about it, one day, when there's more time.

MIMI: Can I ask you a question? Something that I wonder about? Did Uncle Pedro kill himself, was it suicide? Did Grandpa have mistresses?

MIRIAM: How do you know?

MIMI: Information slips out in the middle of a fight.

MIRIAM: He drank himself to death.

MIMI: Oh, I thought he did it violently.

MIRIAM: And your grandpa had a whole whorehouse full of wives.

Mimi and Miriam laugh.

MIMI: I'm like Grandpa. I'm pregnant . . .

MIRIAM: Don't kid me.

MIMI: Aunt Miriam, I am.

MIRIAM: Oh God.

MIMI: What are you doing?

MIRIAM: I need this. *(She takes a valium)* Don't you use a pill?

MIMI: With my mother.

MIRIAM: I don't understand.

MIMI: She'd kill me.

MIRIAM: True. Why did you do it?

MIMI: Freedom.

MIRIAM: Stupidity.

MIMI: Will you help me?

Oscar enters.

MIRIAM: My God, a movie star.

OSCAR: No, just your nephew, Oscar.

MIRIAM: Your hair is combed. You cut your fingernails?

OSCAR: Better than that, a manicure. You two look sexy today.

MIRIAM: Thank you. She's not a virgin . . .

OSCAR: So?

MIMI: I'm pregnant—

MIRIAM: Don't tell him.

OSCAR: Oh, Mimi.

MIRIAM: What are you going to do?

OSCAR: Pretend she didn't say it. Poor Mimi.

MIMI: You're no saint.

OSCAR: I'm not pregnant.

MIMI: Not because you haven't tried.

OSCAR: Oh, I love *you.*

Manuela enters.

MIRIAM: You better not talk.

MANUELA: You're here. Good.

MIMI: If you tell her, I'll tell her you're a fruit.

OSCAR: I don't care.

MIMI: Swear.

OSCAR: I swear.

MANUELA: You look beautiful. Here, sit on my lap.

Oscar sits on Manuela's lap.

MIRIAM: He'll get wrinkled.

MIMI: This is revolting.

MANUELA: I promised your mother that we will be polite.

MIMI: The slut is not coming.

OSCAR: Good. A curse on Argentina.

MANUELA: Oscar, if you ever see her, it is your duty to kick her in the ass. But be good to your father today. It's not his fault. We all know that your father is a decent man. We all know that she got control of him with as they say "powders."

MIMI: I think they call it "blowing."

MANUELA: Blowing? She blowed-up his ego, is that what you think?

MIMI: Right.

MANUELA: No. You are wrong. She did it with drugs. But your mother wants you not to fight with your father. She wants him back.

OSCAR: I'll have to react however I feel.

MANUELA: Your mother is weak and she cannot take another emotional scene. And these Jewish people that Lizette is marrying would never understand about witchcraft, after all they don't even believe in Christ.

OSCAR: I can't promise anything.

MANUELA: Today will be a happy day. Lizette is marrying a nice boy, he's buying her a house. And your mother has a plan.

OSCAR: Right . . .

MANUELA: Right, Miriam?

MIRIAM: You're right. But if I ever see that Argentinian.

MANUELA: You're going to be a good girl, right, Mimi?

MIMI: I'll do whatever the team decides.

OSCAR: Spoken like a true American.

SONIA *(Enters)*: You made it in time for the pictures, thank God.

OSCAR: Do I have to pose with Dad?

SONIA: No fights.

OSCAR: All right. But I'm standing next to you.

SONIA: Thank you. Miriam, Mama, they want more pictures with you. And in ten minutes "The Family Portrait."

MIMI: That'll be a sight.

MANUELA: Is my hair all right?

SONIA: Yes. Here, put on your corsage.

BROKEN EGGS

MANUELA: Thank you.

MIRIAM: And for me?

SONIA: The gardenias.

Miriam and Manuela exit.

You look neat, Oscar. Thank God. The photographer suggested a family portrait, the entire family. He said it will be something we will cherish forever.

OSCAR: Why?

Osvaldo enters.

SONIA: Well, the family portrait will be a record, proof that we were really a family. That we really existed, Oscar. Oscar, my father's name.

OSCAR: I'm glad you named me after him and not Osvaldo.

SONIA: At first I thought of naming you after your father, but then I thought, "That's so old-fashioned, it's 1951, time for something new."

OSCAR: Good for you.

MIMI: What a sign of liberation.

OSVALDO: Oh?!

OSCAR: So . . . continue, Mama.

SONIA: You like the story?

OSCAR: Yes.

SONIA: You, Mimi?

MIMI: Fascinating.

SONIA: Well, and since your grandpa has no son, I named you after him.

OSCAR: I bet he liked that.

SONIA: It made him very happy. I keep thinking he'll show up today. He'll walk in soon, my father. "Papa, do you like it?" And he would say . . .

MIMI: "We have to get back to Cuba."

OSCAR: "We have to fight!"

MIMI: "Where papayas grow as large as watermelons and guayabas and mangoes grow on trees. How could anyone starve in a place like that?"

OSVALDO: Then someone took it all away.

OSCAR: He had everything. He had pride, honor—

OSVALDO: True but someone took it away.

OSCAR: That doesn't matter.

OSVALDO: Well, it does, he lost.

SONIA: You loved him, I know you did, everyone did.

OSVALDO: Yes, right, I did.

OSCAR: He fought and he knew what he believed in. He knew what his life was about.

OSVALDO: Maybe that's why he wanted to die.

SONIA: No, just a stroke.

Pause.

OSCAR: Daddy, do you like my suit?

OSVALDO: Well, it's really a sports coat and pants.

OSCAR: It's linen.

OSVALDO: It'll wrinkle.

OSCAR: I wanted to look nice.

SONIA: It does.

OSVALDO: It doesn't matter.

OSCAR: No, I don't suppose it really does.

OSVALDO: It means nothing.

OSCAR: What means something, Daddy?

OSVALDO: Columns that add up, neatly. Formulas where the answer is always guaranteed!

OSCAR: Guarantees mean something?!

OSVALDO: The answer. That's what means something.

OSCAR: Then I have a meaningless life.

OSVALDO: Stop it.

OSCAR: I never found any answers.

OSVALDO: Stop your melodrama.

OSCAR: I'm going to pretend you didn't say that. I'm twenty-eight years old and I refuse to get involved with you in the emotional ways that you used to abuse our relationship.

MIMI: Time for a Cuba Libre. *(She exits)*

OSVALDO: How much did that piece of dialogue cost me?

OSCAR: Let's stop.

OSVALDO: From which quack did you get that from?

OSCAR: From the one that told me you were in the closet.

OSVALDO: What closet?

Sonia goes to check if anyone's listening.

OSCAR: It's an expression they have in America for men who are afraid, no, they question, no, who fears that he wants to suck cock.

BROKEN EGGS

Osvaldo slaps Oscar.

OSVALDO: Control yourself, learn to control your tongue!

OSCAR: Did that one hit home?

OSVALDO: Spoiled brat.

OSCAR: Takes one to know one. God, I despise you.

OSVALDO: I'm ashamed of you, you're such a nervous wreck, all those doctors, all the money I spend.

OSCAR: Thanks, Daddy, I had such a fine example of Manhood from you.

OSVALDO: Bum!

OSCAR: Fool.

SONIA: No psychology today! You're both the same, you're both so selfish, think of Lizette, her fiancé's family, what if they hear this. Quiet!

OSCAR: Leave us alone.

SONIA: No. I belong in this argument too, I'm the mother and the wife.

OSCAR: The ex-wife, Mama.

SONIA: No, in this particular triangle, the wife.

OSCAR *(To Sonia)*: Your life is a failure.

OSVALDO: Because of you.

SONIA: Don't say that, Osvaldo. He's our son.

OSVALDO: He's just like you.

SONIA: What do you mean by that?!

OSVALDO: An emotional wreck.

OSCAR: That's better than being emotionally dead.

OSVALDO: I hate him.

SONIA: No. Osvaldo, how dare you! *(She cries)*

OSCAR: See what you've made, turned her into?!

OSVALDO: It's because of you.

SONIA: I refuse to be the cause of this fight, today we're having a wedding, so both of you smile.

OSVALDO: You're right, Sonia, I'm sorry.

OSCAR: God.

SONIA: I'm going to be with Lizette. You two control yourselves.

OSCAR *(Whispers)*: Faggot.

Sonia exits.

Sissy.

OSVALDO: I bet you know all about that?!

OSCAR: Yes, want to hear about it?

Alfredo enters.

OSVALDO: Not in front of your grandfather.

OSCAR: There's no way to talk to you, you petty bastard. *(He starts to cry)*

OSVALDO: Exactly like her, crying.

OSCAR *(Stops crying)*: Because we were both unfortunate enough to have to know you in an intimate way.

OSVALDO: Other people don't feel that way.

OSCAR: That's because they're made of ice. A lot of Nazis in Argentina.

OSVALDO: Your sister needs me today. I'm going to make sure she's happy. Men don't cry. Now stop it. *(He exits)*

OSCAR: Right.

ALFREDO: Be careful.

OSCAR: About what?

ALFREDO: You show too much. Be on your guard.

OSCAR: So what?

ALFREDO: You let him see too much of you.

OSCAR: He's my father.

ALFREDO: He's a man first, my son second, your father third.

OSCAR: That's how he feels? He told you that? Did he?!

ALFREDO: Be a little more like me. And a little less like your other grandfather. He's dead. I'm still alive.

OSCAR: He was ill. It wasn't his fault.

ALFREDO: He was a fool.

OSCAR: No. That's not true.

ALFREDO: He was foolish. He trusted mankind. Money made him flabby. He thought if you gave a starving man a plate of food, he thanks you. He didn't know that he also resents you, he also waits. No one wants to beg for food, it's humiliating.

OSCAR: Of course no one wants to.

ALFREDO: So they wait. And when they regain their strength, they stab you in the back.

OSCAR: How can you think that's true?!

ALFREDO: We are the proof of my theory—Cubans. He did it to us—Fidel, our neighbors, everybody. So never feed a hungry man.

OSCAR: You don't really believe that.

MIMI *(Enters)*: The picture, Grandpa. Oscar, the family portrait!

ALFREDO: I'm on my way. Comb your hair. Fix your tie. Your suit is already wrinkled.

OSCAR: Real linen does that.

Alfredo exits with Mimi. Oscar takes out a bottle of cocaine—the kind that premeasures a hit. He goes outside but leaves the entrance door open. He snorts.

Ah, breakfast.

Oscar snorts again. Osvaldo enters but does not see Oscar. He goes straight to the bar, comes back with a drink—a J&B double—and gulps it down. He looks at the corsages. We hear Oscar sniffing coke.

OSVALDO *(To himself)*: White, compete with the bride . . . very funny, Sonia.

SONIA *(Enters)*: Osvaldo, we are waiting for you. The family portrait, come.

OSVALDO: No, I can't face them.

SONIA: Don't be silly.

OSVALDO: They love you. They hate me, my sister, my father, my children, they all hate me.

SONIA: They don't. No one hates their own family. It's a sin to hate people in your immediate family.

OSVALDO: They always hated me. Till I was seventeen I thought—

SONIA: That they had found you in a trash can, I know, Osvaldo. We need a record, a family portrait. The last one was taken at Oscar's seventh birthday. It's time for a new one.

OSVALDO: You don't need me.

SONIA: It wouldn't be one without you.

OSVALDO: For who?

SONIA: For everybody. Be brave. Take my hand. I won't bite.

Osvaldo holds her hand.

After all, I'm the mother and you are the father of the bride.

OSCAR *(Sticks his head in)*: The Argentinian just drove up.

OSVALDO: Liar.

OSCAR: She looks drunk.

OSVALDO: Liar.

OSCAR: What do they drink in Argentina?

SONIA: Behave!

A car starts honking.

OSCAR: Sounds like your car.

OSVALDO: How dare she. How can she humiliate me. How can she disobey me.

SONIA: Oscar, go out and say your father is posing with his past family. Tell her that after the portrait is taken, she can come in.

OSCAR: But she has to sit in the back.

SONIA: No, I'm going to be polite. That's what I was taught.

OSVALDO: Go and tell her.

OSCAR: Remember, Mama, I did it for you. (He exits)

OSVALDO: Thank you. Hold my hand.

SONIA: Kiss me.

OSVALDO: Here?

SONIA: Yes, today I'm the mother and the wife.

Osvaldo and Sonia kiss.

OSVALDO: You did a good job.

SONIA: You do like it?

OSVALDO: I mean with our daughters. They're good girls . . . like their mother.

SONIA: They have a good father.

OSVALDO: That's true.

Osvaldo and Sonia exit, Oscar reenters.

OSCAR: The family portrait? This family. . . . My family. The Father, Jesus Christ his only son and the Holy Ghost (Crossing himself) . . . why the *fuck* did you send me to this family.

Blackout.

END OF ACT ONE

BROKEN EGGS

ACT TWO

Afternoon. Offstage, the band is playing "Snow," an Argentinian folksong, and a woman is singing. Miriam is in the phone booth. Mimi is looking at the bridal bouquet and pulling it apart. Sonia enters eating cake.

WOMAN'S VOICE *(Singing offstage):*
Don't sing brother, don't sing,
I hear Moscow is covered with snow.
And the wolves run away out of hunger.
Don't sing 'cause Olga's not coming.

Even if the sun shines again.
Even if the snow falls again.
Even if the sun shines again.
Even if the snow falls again.

Walking to Siberia tomorrow, oh,
Out goes the caravan,
Who knows if the sun
Will light our march of horror.

While in Moscow, my Olga, perhaps,
To another, her love she surrenders.
Don't sing brothers, don't sing.
For God's sake, oh God, no.

United by chains to the steppes
A thousand leagues we'll go walking.
Walking to Siberia, no.
Don't sing, I am filled with pain.
And Moscow is covered with snow.
And the snow has entered my soul.
Moscow now covered with snow.
And the snow has entered my soul.

SONIA: It's insult to injury an Argentinian song about going to Siberia, Russia. Moscow is covered with snow . . . what do Argentinians know about Moscow? I wish she'd go to Siberia tomorrow. *(To Mimi)* They are walking a thousand leagues to their exile . . . I took a plane ride ninety-nine miles, a forty-five-minute excursion to my doom.

MIRIAM *(To phone)*: No, shit no! Liars.

SONIA: Don't sing, Sonia . . . *(She sings)* 'cause Moscow is covered with snow, right, Mimi?

MIMI: Right.

SONIA: When I first got here this place looked to me like a farm town. Are you happy, dear?

MIMI: I don't think so.

SONIA: No, say yes!

MIMI: Yes.

SONIA: That's good.

MIMI: Ciao!

Mimi runs to the bathroom to puke. Osvaldo enters.

SONIA: So, you had to play a song for her?

OSVALDO: She told the band she wanted to sing it. But it's the only Argentinian song they know.

SONIA: Good for the band! Remember when we thought Fidel was going to send us to Russia, to Moscow? Siberia, Siberia, this place is like Siberia!

OSVALDO: It's too warm to be Siberia. *(He kisses Sonia passionately)* It was a beautiful ceremony. *(He kisses her again)*

SONIA: Dance with me. Tell them to play a danzón.

OSVALDO: Let's dance in here.

SONIA: She'll get angry? It's our daughter's wedding.

OSVALDO: She's my wife.

SONIA: I was first.

OSVALDO: You're both my wife.

Osvaldo and Sonia dance.

SONIA: Before my sixteenth birthday your family moved to Cojimar . . . your cousin brought you to the club.

OSVALDO: You were singing a Rita Hayworth song called "Put the Blame on . . . Me"?

SONIA: No, "Mame" . . . I was imitating her . . . did I look ridiculous?

OSVALDO: No!

SONIA *(Starts to do Rita's number, substituting "Cuban" for "Frisco")*:
Put the blame on Mame, boys
Put the blame on Mame

BROKEN EGGS

One night she started to shim and shake
That began the Cuban quake
So-o-o, put the blame on Mame, boys
Put the blame on Mame . . .

OSVALDO: You look sexy.

SONIA: I let you kiss me, then you became part of the club.

OSVALDO: On your seventeenth birthday I married you.

SONIA: Well, I kissed you.

OSVALDO: Was I the only one?

SONIA: Yes.

OSVALDO: And by your eighteenth birthday we had Oscar. I should go back to the party. She'll start looking for me.

SONIA: Tell her to relax. Tell the band to stop playing that stupid song. I want to dance. I want more Cuban music.

OSVALDO: All right! What song?

SONIA: "Guantanamera."

OSVALDO: They might know "Babalú."

SONIA: That's an American song.

Manuela and Alfredo enter, in the middle of a conversation. Osvaldo exits to the ballroom. Sonia goes outside.

MANUELA: The trouble is Americans are weak . . . they don't know how to make decisions.

ALFREDO: At least they are happy—

MANUELA: Why?

ALFREDO: Money!

MANUELA: You had that in Cuba, Alfredo, but—

ALFREDO: Look at my son—he has an accounting firm—

MANUELA: He's only a partner.

ALFREDO: He has a Lincoln Continental, a classy car; two beautiful houses, with pools and—

MANUELA: Don't talk about the prostitute's house in front of me, Alfredo, please.

ALFREDO: Forgive me.

MANUELA: We knew how to make decisions, we—

ALFREDO: Of course.

MANUELA: Fight who you don't agree with, do not doubt that you are right, and if they use force, you use force, bullets if you have to. Only right and wrong, no middle, not like Americans always asking questions, always in the middle, always maybe. Sometimes I think those Democrats are Communists—

ALFREDO: No, Manuela, you see in demo—

MANUELA: Democracy, Communism, the two don't go together, at least the Russians know that much. They don't let people complain in Russia, but here, anybody can do anything.

The band is playing "Guantanamera."

At last some good music, no more of that Argentinian shit. *(She hums some of the song)*

ALFREDO: That's one of my favorite songs.

MANUELA: Yes, beautiful.

ALFREDO: May I have this dance?

MANUELA: Yes . . . but do I remember how?

MIMI *(Who has reentered)*: It'll come back to you, Grandma.

Manuela, Alfredo and Mimi exit to the dance floor. Miriam is still sitting in the phone booth, smoking. Sonia enters. Miriam opens the phone-booth doors.

MIRIAM: I just made a phone call to Cuba, and you can.

SONIA: They got you through?

MIRIAM: Yes. The overseas operator said, "Sometimes they answer, but only if they feel like it."

SONIA: Who did you call?

MIRIAM: My . . . our house. . . . I sometimes think that I live at the same time there as here. That I left a dual spirit there. When I go to a funeral I look through the windows as I drive and the landscapes I see are the streets outside the cemetery in Guanabacoa, not Miami. A while ago I looked out at the dance floor and I thought I was in the ballroom back home. That's why I had to call. I miss the floor, the windows, the air, the roof.

SONIA: The house is still standing, though, it is still there.

MIRIAM: But we are not.

SONIA: I saw a picture of it. It hasn't been painted in twenty years, we painted it last.

MIRIAM: Sonia, she said upstairs he's crying again.

SONIA: You're sending chills up my spine.

BROKEN EGGS

MIRIAM: Is it Pedro crying?

SONIA: No, she was trying to scare you. We have to hold on to it, to the way we remember it, painted.

MIRIAM: I think I heard Pedro screaming in the garden before she hung up.

SONIA: No, he's dead, he went to heaven.

MIRIAM: No, he's in hell. If there's a heaven he's in hell. Suicides go to hell. He was the only one that managed to remain, death keeps him there. Maybe the house filled with strangers is his hell.

SONIA: Why he did it I'll never understand. Maybe he had to die for us?

MIRIAM: No, he didn't do it for *me*.

SONIA: Maybe that's the way things are, maybe one of us had to die. Maybe there's an order to all these things.

MIRIAM: There's no order to things, don't you know that by now? It's chaos, only chaos.

Mimi enters.

SONIA: No, there's a more important reason, that's why he did it.

MIMI: What?

SONIA: This conversation is not for your ears.

MIMI: Why not?

Lizette enters.

SONIA: Because it isn't, that's all.

LIZETTE: Mama! Daddy started dancing with her and Oscar's whistling at them, whispering "Puta, putica."

MIRIAM: The Americans won't understand what they are saying.

LIZETTE: Americans know what "puta" means. My husband is embarrassed. Other people get divorces and don't act like this. Tell him he must stop. No name-calling in Spanish or in English. This is a bilingual state.

MIMI: No, Mama, don't do it.

MIRIAM: Mimi's right, let them do whatever they want.

SONIA: Right, why should I protect her?

LIZETTE: How about me? Who's going to protect me?

SONIA: Your husband.

MIMI: Tell him to tell them to stop, you've got your husband now, your own little family unit.

LIZETTE: Fuck off, Mimi. I'm begging you, Mama, please. Just take him to the side and tell him to leave her alone, to let her have a good time.

SONIA: To let her have a good time?!

MIMI: I'll take care of it. *(She yells out to the ballroom)* Hey you slut, Miss Argentina. Don't use my sister's wedding for your crap. Come in here and fight it out with us!

MIRIAM: Mimi, she's flipping the bird at you. She's gesturing fuck you.

MIMI: Fuck yourself!

LIZETTE: Mama! Stop her! Oh God—

MIRIAM *(Yells to the ballroom)*: You're just a bitch, lady.

LIZETTE *(Starts to cry)*: Oh, God, oh, God—

SONIA: In a little while everybody will forget about it—

LIZETTE: Oh God, Mama. Everybody's looking at us. They are so embarrassed. You let them ruin my wedding. You promised. I hate you. It's a fiasco. I hate you, Mimi.

SONIA: Sorry, promises are something nobody keeps, including me.

LIZETTE: You're such assholes.

SONIA: Everybody's got their faults, learn to live with it!

LIZETTE: You failed me.

MIMI: That was great, Aunt Miriam.

SONIA: I'm sorry.

MIRIAM: Thanks, Mimi, it was fun.

OSVALDO *(Enters)*: How could you . . .

MIRIAM: Careful!

OSVALDO: Help me, Sonia.

SONIA: Osvaldo, I've put up with a lot.

OSVALDO: How about me? I want you and your children to apologize to her.

SONIA: No.

MIMI: Never.

MIRIAM: She should leave the party and let the rest of us have a good time. What the hell is she doing here?

OSVALDO: For my sake, Sonia.

SONIA: I'm sorry, I can't.

OSVALDO: What am I going to do?

SONIA: Who do you love, me?

OSVALDO: Yes.

SONIA: Who do you love, her?

OSVALDO: Yes.

SONIA: So full of contradictions, so confused. I'll go tell her that. He loves both of us, Cuba and Argentina!

OSVALDO: This is not the time to kid me, look at Lizette, she's upset.

LIZETTE: I'll never be able to talk to my mother-in-law again.

MIRIAM: It's your fault, Osvaldo. He never moved from the garden.

OSVALDO: Miriam?! Who never moved from the garden?

MIRIAM: Pedro. He never left the garden.

OSVALDO: None of us have.

MIRIAM: He stayed. He took a razor blade but remained locked forever in our family's garden.

OSVALDO: He was a coward.

MIRIAM: Maybe you are the coward, you keep running away.

OSVALDO: From what?

OSCAR (Enters, trying not to laugh): I'm sorry. I behaved badly.

OSVALDO: Tell me, Miriam, from what? (He exits)

OSCAR: Don't cry, Lizette, forgive me? Hmm?

LIZETTE: Oscar, now they're starting to fight about Cuba. I just want to cry. They're going to tell my husband, "Your wife is from a crazy family. Are you sure she's not mentally disturbed?"

MIMI: Are you sure you're not mentally disturbed?

Mimi and Oscar laugh. Osvaldo reenters.

OSVALDO: What do I run away from that he faced?

MIRIAM: That we lost everything.

SONIA: Everything, no.

OSVALDO: You think I don't know that?

MIRIAM: Pedro knew. He became invisible but remains in silence, as proof.

OSVALDO: As proof of what?

SONIA: That we are not a very nice family? Is that what you are saying?

OSVALDO: He had nothing to do with us, he was an alcoholic.

SONIA: He killed himself because of our sins.

OSVALDO: No, Sonia, that was Christ, Pedro was a drunk, not a Christ figure.

MIRIAM: Because of our lies, Sonia.

OSVALDO: What lies?

MIRIAM: Why did you desert him? You, his brother, you were the only one he spoke to, the only one he needed.

OSVALDO: He made me sick.

MIRIAM: You were always together, you always spent your days together.

OSVALDO: He was an alcoholic.

MIRIAM: We were all alcoholics.

SONIA: I was never an alcoholic.

MIRIAM: He needed you.

OSVALDO: He was perverted.

MIRIAM: We were all perverted. That's why the new society got rid of us.

OSVALDO: Our mother is not perverted!

MIRIAM: No, just insane.

SONIA: No, she's an honest woman, now your father—

OSVALDO: My father was just selfish, he had too many mistresses.

SONIA: Fifteen.

OSCAR: Fifteen?

MIMI: All at once?

LIZETTE: Who gives a fuck? Everybody in this family is a—

MIRIAM: I'm the one that suffered from that, not you, Osvaldo. You take after Daddy so don't complain. Why did you let Pedro kill himself?

OSVALDO: He wanted too much from me.

MIRIAM: He needed you.

OSVALDO: He wanted my mind, he wanted my . . ., my . . ., he wanted everything.

MIRIAM: You're glad he did it?

OSVALDO: I was relieved.

MIRIAM: He knew too much, ha!

SONIA: Too much of what?

MIRIAM: The perversions.

SONIA: What perversions?

MIRIAM: Too much about his perversions, darling Sonia, you married a corrupted family, you really deserved better.

OSCAR: Uh-huh.

LIZETTE: I'm closing the door.

Manuela and Alfredo enter.

MANUELA: I'll never forget what he said.

ALFREDO: When?

MANUELA: In 1959, after the son-of-a-bitch's first speech, he said, "That boy is going to be trouble . . . he's full of Commie ideals."

ALFREDO: I must say I did not suspect it. I was so bored with Batista's bullshit I thought, a revolution, good. We'll get rid of the bums, the loafers, but instead, they got rid of us.

BROKEN EGGS

MANUELA: I hope he rots. Rot, Fidel Castro, die of cancer of the balls.

ALFREDO: Let's hope.

MANUELA: Then they came. And they took our businesses away, one by one. And we had to let them do it. They took over each of them, one after the other. It took the milicianos three days. I looked at Oscar while they did it, for him it was like they . . . for him, that was his life's work, he felt like . . .

OSCAR: Like they were plucking out his heart. Like they were sticking pins into his brain. Like they were having birds peck out his genitals. Like he was being betrayed.

MANUELA: Yes, that's it.

ALFREDO: I hate myself for helping them, bastards.

MANUELA: All he wanted after that was—

SONIA: To fight back.

OSCAR: Right.

MIRIAM: I still do. I still want to fight somebody!

SONIA: But he did fight back. Till the day he died, he never gave up. Right, Mama?

MANUELA: "We are in an emergency," that's how he put it, "an emergency."

MIRIAM: Daddy. Daddy, I am in an emergency now. I have taken six valiums and it's only noon.

ALFREDO: Why?

MIRIAM: Because I want to strangle you every time I look at you.

LIZETTE: Quiet, they're going to want an annulment.

MANUELA: My God, Miriam!

OSCAR: Who?

ALFREDO: Why?

MIRIAM: Why?!

LIZETTE: The Jews, they're a quiet people.

ALFREDO: Yes, Miriam, why?

MIRIAM: Why did you send your mistresses' daughters to my school?!

MANUELA: Miriam, not in front of the children.

ALFREDO: Because it was a good school.

MIRIAM: People in my class wouldn't talk to me because of you!

ALFREDO: Sorry.

OSVALDO: Sorry? That's all you have to say to her?! That's the only answer you give?!

ALFREDO: I don't know, what else should I say?

OSVALDO: Why did you not once congratulate me for finishing the university?! Why did you let me drink? Why did you let Pedro drink?

ALFREDO: I never noticed that you drank.

MIMI: Why did you leave my mother, and leave me . . . and never came to see me play volleyball?

OSVALDO: Leave me alone, I'm talking to my father.

MIMI: And who are you to me?

MANUELA: Good girl, good question.

OSVALDO: You? Why did you make your daughter think that the only person in the world who deserved her love was your husband?!

MANUELA: He was strong.

OSVALDO: He got drunk. He was a coward when he died.

OSCAR: No. That's not true.

MANUELA: He was a real man. What are you?

LIZETTE: You mean old hag, don't you ever talk to my dad again like—

SONIA: Don't you ever call your grandmother that. She's my mother!

LIZETTE: I'm going back to the wedding. (*She exits*)

OSCAR: Why did they kick us out?

Silence.

OSVALDO: We left. We wanted to leave.

OSCAR: No one asked me.

SONIA: We had to protect you from them.

MIRIAM: That's right.

OSVALDO: They wanted to brainwash you, to turn you into a Communist.

OSCAR: No one explained it to me. You told me I was coming here for the weekend.

OSVALDO: It was not up to you.

SONIA: You were just a child, it was up to us.

OSVALDO: That's right.

MIRIAM: And we made the right decision, believe me.

OSCAR: Miriam, why did you let me be locked out? That day in Miami, November, 1962. The day the guy from the Jehovah's Witnesses came to see you. And you took him to your room to discuss the end of the world.

MIRIAM: It was a joke. I was only twenty. I don't believe in God.

OSCAR: Well, you locked me out. And I sat outside and you laughed at me, and I sat there by a tree and I wanted to die. I wanted to kill myself at the age of ten. I wanted to beat my head against the tree, and I thought, "Please stop working, brain, even they locked me out, even my family, not just my country, my family too." Bastards! Fidel was right. If I had a gun, I'd shoot you. I curse you, you shits. Who asked me?

OSVALDO: The revolution had nothing to do with you. You don't *really* remember it, and believe it or not, it did not happen just for you, Oscar.

OSCAR: Yeah, I didn't notice you damaged.

OSVALDO: I had to go to the market at age thirty-two and shop for the first time in my life.

MIMI: So what?

OSCAR: God.

OSVALDO: And I could not tell what fruit was ripe and what fruit was not ripe. I did not know how to figure that out. I cried at the Food King market in Canoga Park. Some people saw me. *(He cries)*

OSCAR: Big deal.

OSVALDO *(Stops crying)*: And Sonia, you refused to come and help me! You made me go do it alone. And shopping is the wife's duty.

SONIA: I couldn't. I felt weak. I was pregnant with Mimi. I'm sorry, Osvaldo. *(To Oscar)* I wanted you to live a noble life.

OSCAR: How?

SONIA: I don't know. I taught you not to put your elbows on the table. You had perfect eating habits . . .

OSCAR: What does that have to do with nobility?

SONIA: It shows you're not common. That's noble.

OSCAR: No, Mama, nobility—

SONIA: Yes.

OSCAR: No, nobility has to do with caring about the ugly things, seeing trash and loving it. It has to do with compassion, not table manners. It has to do with thought, not what people think about you.

SONIA: Stop picking on me.

OSCAR: I'm not picking on you.

SONIA: Everybody is always picking on me. I failed, I know I failed.

OSCAR: No, you just don't try. Why don't you try?

SONIA: Try what?

OSCAR: To do something.

SONIA: No.

OSCAR: Why?

SONIA: I'm not some whore that can go from guy to guy.

OSVALDO: Are you talking about my wife?

OSCAR: Try it.

SONIA: Don't insult me. Stop insulting me.

OSCAR: You need somebody.

SONIA: Stop it!

OSVALDO: Leave her alone.

Osvaldo grabs Sonia. They walk towards the ballroom, then stop. We hear the band playing "Que Sera, Sera."

MANUELA: I think they're going to dance.

MIRIAM: I want to see the Argentinian's expression.

Sonia and Osvaldo are now dancing. The others watch. Mimi and Oscar go into the phone booth to snort coke.

ALFREDO: Leave all three of them alone. *(He goes outside to smoke a cigar)*

Miriam and Manuela walk past Sonia and Osvaldo toward the ballroom.

MIRIAM: Why are you dancing out in the hall . . . afraid of Argentina?

Miriam and Manuela exit.

OSVALDO: I'd like to take a big piece of wood and beat some sense into her. . . . No, I want to beat her to death!

SONIA: She went too far . . . she lost control . . . she gets excited.

OSVALDO: They always lose control. Pedro thought there was no limit . . . that you did not have to stop anywhere . . . life was a whim. . . . But I knew that you have to stop yourself . . . that's being civilized, that's what makes us different than dogs . . . you can't have everything you feel you want . . .

SONIA: He was a tortured soul . . . and you loved him . . .

OSVALDO: My big brother. *(He starts to cry)*

SONIA: And you tried to help him . . .

OSVALDO: How?

SONIA: The only way you knew how, with affection.

OSVALDO: Affection?

SONIA: Yes, and that's decent.

OSVALDO: Maybe it is. Maybe I am.

Sonia and Osvaldo kiss. He takes her out to the dance floor. She smiles. Oscar and Mimi come out of the phone booth. Oscar continues to snort cocaine.

OSCAR: He did it. Well, at least he had the balls to take her out and dance. She won. You see if you have a plan and follow it . . . *(Sniff, sniff)* ah, hurray for the American dream.

MIMI: It's pathetic. They're still dancing. Oh God help us, she believes anything he tells her.

OSCAR: She had to endure too many things.

MIMI: What, losing her maid?

OSCAR: They never tell her the truth.

MIMI: And you do? You tell her the truth? Well, I'm gonna tell her.

OSCAR: I think you should get an abortion.

MIMI: Why should I?

OSCAR: To protect her.

MIMI: Why should I protect her.

OSCAR: I don't know. Lie to her. Tell Dad.

MIMI: Never mind. Pour me some more champagne.

Lizette enters.

I hope one of those horny Cubans just off the boat is ready to rock and roll.

LIZETTE: No more scenes, Mimi. Dad and Mom are enough.

Mimi toasts Lizette with champagne.

MIMI: Arrivederci. *(She exits)*

LIZETTE: They're out there dancing like they were in love or something—

OSCAR: Maybe they are.

LIZETTE: Never, he's being polite and she's showing off. And the Argentinian is complaining to me. And I don't want any part of any of you.

OSCAR: You don't! You think your husband is going to take you away from all this. Does he know about the suicides, how they drink till they explode . . . the violence we live with, the razor blades, the guns, the hangings, the one woman in our family who set herself on fire while her three kids watched?

ALFREDO *(Who has reentered)*: We are just hot-blooded and passionate, that's all.

OSCAR: Grandpa told me a week before . . . "Oscar," he told me . . . "they'll tell you soon I'm in the hospital. That means that I'm on my way out . . . this life here is ridiculous."

ALFREDO: Oscar Hernandez was a fool. That's a fool's kind of suicide, that's what I told you.

OSCAR: A lot of drinks when your blood pressure is high is not a fool's kind of suicide, it's just suicide. Despair, that's always the story of people that get kicked out, that have to find refuge, you and me . . . us.

LIZETTE: No, you. Everybody dies on the day that they're supposed to. Forget about it.

OSCAR: How can I?

ALFREDO: You better teach yourself to.

OSCAR: How can I? Have you taught yourself? Tell me, why do you want to live? For what?

ALFREDO: Because of me . . . here or over there, I still need me!

OSCAR: You don't have any honor.

ALFREDO: Honor for what?

OSCAR: For our country.

ALFREDO: That little island? . . . Look, Oscar, when Columbus first found it there were Indians there, imagine, Indians. So we eliminated the Indians, burned all of them, cleaned up the place. . . . We needed somebody to do the Indians' work so we bought ourselves slaves . . . and then the Spaniards, that's us, and the slaves started to . . . well, you know.

OSCAR: I can only imagine.

ALFREDO: Well, then we started calling ourselves natives. Cubans.

LIZETTE: That's right, a name they made up!

ALFREDO: Right! And we became a nation . . .

OSCAR: A race.

ALFREDO: Yes. And then the U.S. came and liked it, and bought and cheated their way into this little place. They told us (He imitates a Texan accent) "Such a pretty place you have, a valuable piece of real estate. We will help you!" So, they bought us.

OSCAR: We should have eliminated them!

ALFREDO: Maybe. But, what we did . . . was sell it to them and fight against each other for decades, trying to have control of what was left of this pretty place, this valuable piece of real estate. And a bearded guy on a hill talked to us about liberty, and justice, and humanity and humility—and we bought his story. And he took everything away from everybody. And we were forced to end up here. So, we bought their real estate. Do you know how Miami was built?

LIZETTE: With sand that they shipped in from Cojimar! Right?

ALFREDO: That's right. And your other grandfather could not accept the fact that it was just real estate. So he got drunk when he knew he had high blood pressure. What a fool.

LIZETTE: He tells the truth, Oscar.

OSCAR: And Mama thinks it was her country. And someday she'd go back. And I hoped it was my country. What a laugh, huh?

LIZETTE: If you ever tell Mama this, it'll kill her.

OSCAR: Maybe it wouldn't.

LIZETTE: She can't deal with real life, believe me. I'm her daughter, I know what she's really like.

OSCAR: And you can deal with everything?

LIZETTE: Sure. I grew up here, I have a Jewish name now . . . Mrs. Rifkin, that's my name.

OSCAR: Well, Mrs. Rifkin, I'm jealous of you.

ALFREDO: Time for a dance. I haven't danced with the mother of the groom. *(He exits)*

LIZETTE: Try to get away, Mrs. Rifkin!

OSCAR: And the new Mrs. Rifkin is running away. You got away.

LIZETTE: Don't be jealous, Oscar. It's still all back here. *(She points to her brain)*

OSVALDO *(Enters)*: One o'clock, Lizette.

LIZETTE: One more dance.

OSCAR: Why do you have to leave so soon?

LIZETTE: It's another two thousand for the entire day.

OSCAR: God.

OSVALDO: God what?

OSCAR: You have no class.

SONIA *(Enters)*: Osvaldo, I have to talk to you.

OSVALDO: Why?

SONIA: Please, just do me a favor. I have to talk to you.

LIZETTE: Want to dance?

OSCAR: All right.

Lizette and Oscar exit.

OSVALDO: What do you want, Sonia? Tell me, sweetheart.

SONIA (*Hysterical*): Don't be angry at me, there's no more wedding cake, we've run out of wedding cake. There's no more, nothing, no more wedding cake.

OSVALDO: That's all right, we should start getting them out. Tell them to start passing out the packages of rice.

SONIA: No, some people are asking for wedding cake. What do we do? What?

OSVALDO: They've had plenty to eat, a great lunch, a salad, chicken cacciatore, a pastry, all they could drink, champagne, coffee. Tell them to pass out the rice, get this over with, and let's go home.

SONIA: At a wedding, wedding cake is something people expect. I can't embarrass the groom's family again. What do we do, what are you going to do?!

OSVALDO: Let's go up to people we know . . .

SONIA: Only Cubans!

OSVALDO: All right, let's go up to all the Cubans we know and ask them not to eat the cake. Then serve it to the Jews. The Cubans won't care.

SONIA: You do it, I can't. I can't face them.

OSVALDO: No, do it, with me, come on.

Oscar enters. He is about to eat a piece of cake. Sonia grabs it away from him.

OSCAR: What are you doing?

SONIA: You can't eat it, there's not enough.

OSCAR: Why?

OSVALDO: Just do what your mother says. Please, let's go.

SONIA: You do it.

OSVALDO: You're not coming with me?

SONIA: No, I'm sorry. I can't, I'm too embarrassed.

Osvaldo exits.

OSCAR: Okay, give it back to me now.

SONIA: No, take it to that man over there.

OSCAR: Why should I?

SONIA: He didn't get any cake. I think the waiters stole one of the layers. You take it to him. I think his name is Mr. Cohen, the man who's looking at us.

OSCAR: All right. Who?

SONIA (*Points discreetly*): The bald man.

OSCAR: Great.

Manuela and Miriam enter.

MANUELA: Oh my God; Jesus, Sonia. Osvaldo just told me that we are out of cake.

OSCAR: We are. *(He exits)*

MANUELA: We were winning.

SONIA: The stupid waiters cut the pieces too big, Mama.

MANUELA: Americans! This is one of the great follies of my life.

SONIA: Of course, Mama, this is worse than the revolution.

Manuela goes outside.

MIRIAM: No, in the revolution people died.

SONIA: They really did, didn't they?

MIRIAM: Real blood was shed, real Cuban blood.

SONIA: I forget sometimes.

MIRIAM: Only when I'm calm, that's when I remember, when I'm waking up or when I'm half asleep . . . at those moments.

SONIA: Let's go out to the dance floor and dance like we did at the Tropicana.

LIZETTE *(Enters)*: I ripped my wedding dress.

SONIA: Oh well, dear, it's only supposed to last one day. Maybe the next wedding you go to, Lizette, will be mine.

LIZETTE: Who did you find, Mama?

SONIA: Your father.

LIZETTE: Mama, Daddy can't afford another wife.

SONIA: I'm not another wife, Lizette.

LIZETTE: I hope you are right.

MIRIAM: Wait a minute. *(She gives Lizette five hundred dollars)* In case you decide you need something else when you are on your honeymoon.

LIZETTE: Another five hundred. I think we have three thousand dollars in cash.

Lizette exits to the dressing room. Miriam lights two cigarettes. She gives one to Sonia.

MIRIAM: Let's go. Remember when we thought Fidel looked sexy.

SONIA: Shh.

Miriam and Sonia sashay off to the ballroom. Osvaldo and Alfredo enter. Osvaldo is eating a big piece of cake.

ALFREDO: All women are hysterical.

OSVALDO: I got out there, took the cake from the Cubans, who were outraged. A couple of them called me a Jew. I took it to the Jews and they were as happy as can be. I offered them the cake but nobody wanted any. She made me go through all that for nothing.

ALFREDO: They were being polite, Jews don't like to appear greedy.

OSVALDO *(Eats the cake)*: Well, it's delicious.

ALFREDO: It's Cuban cake.

OSVALDO: The only thing that I like Cuban is the food.

ALFREDO: Then start acting like a man. You have one crying in the back and the other demanding in the front!

OSVALDO: I do.

ALFREDO: You don't have the energy to play it both ways.

OSVALDO: What are you talking about?

ALFREDO: Your wife . . . Sonia!

OSVALDO: She'll never change.

ALFREDO: Why should she?!

OSVALDO: To be acceptable.

Alfredo slaps Osvaldo. Mimi enters.

MIMI: The rice, we have to hit her with the rice.

Osvaldo and Alfredo, glaring at each other, exit with Mimi. Lizette enters in her honeymoon outfit and goes outside. She sees Manuela. They come back in.

LIZETTE: Grandma, you've been in the sun!

MANUELA: I was taking a nap. You know when you get old you need rest.

LIZETTE: You were crying, Grandma. Don't.

MANUELA: We didn't have enough cake!

LIZETTE: Nothing turned out right, Grandma, that's the truth.

MANUELA: You're right. Oscar would have made sure that we had a good time. My husband would have spent more money. I would have been proud. Your mother would have been proud. You would have been proud.

LIZETTE: Grandma, aren't you proud of me?

MANUELA: Yes.

LIZETTE: Did you love each other?

MANUELA: Yes, dear, we did.

LIZETTE: And you never doubted it?

MANUELA: No, dear.

LIZETTE: I hope I can do it. Wish me luck, Grandma. I don't want to fail. I want to be happy.

MANUELA: I hope that you know how to fight. Everything will try to stop and corrupt your life. I hope your husband is successful and that you have enough children.

LIZETTE: And that I never regret my life.

MANUELA: That will be my prayer.

LIZETTE: That if anyone goes, it's me, that I'm the one that walks. That he'll be hooked on me forever.

MANUELA: That's right.

LIZETTE: Thank you.

MANUELA: A beautiful dress. I'll get the rice.

LIZETTE: No, we are sneaking out. I don't want rice all over my clothes. In ten minutes tell them we tricked them, that we got away.

MANUELA: Go. Don't be nervous. Tonight everything will be all right. Don't worry, have a nice vacation.

LIZETTE: It's eighty degrees in Hawaii, it's an island, like Cuba.

MANUELA: Cuba was more beautiful.

Lizette exits.

Then politicians got in the way.

LIZETTE (*Offstage*): Honey, we did it. Give me a kiss.

Manuela goes outside.

ENTIRE CAST (*Offstage*): Ah! Uh-Uh! Noooooooooo!

LIZETTE (*Offstage*): My God, rice, run!

Sonia enters, covered with rice, followed by Osvaldo.

OSVALDO: It was a beautiful wedding.

SONIA: You're coming home with me?

OSVALDO: I can't.

SONIA: Yes, come with me.

OSVALDO: Not tonight.

SONIA: When?

OSVALDO: Never. (*Pause*) Nothing is left between you and me.

SONIA: Nothing?

OSVALDO: Nothing.

SONIA: I'm not even your mistress?

OSVALDO: That's right. Revolutions create hell for all people involved.

SONIA: Don't do this. We belong together, we were thrown out. Discarded. We stayed together, Cubans, we are Cubans. Nothing really came between us.

OSVALDO: Something did for me.

Mimi enters.

SONIA: What about our family? What we swore to Christ?

OSVALDO: I don't believe in anything, not even Christ.

SONIA: And me?

OSVALDO: I have another wife, she's my wife now. I have another life.

SONIA: If I was my father, I'd kill you!

MIMI *(To Osvaldo)*: Your wife is waiting in the car. *(To Sonia)* She told me to tell him.

OSVALDO: Sonia, I'm starting fresh. You should too.

SONIA: I should, yes, I should. *(She takes out the bottle that Manuela gave her in Act One and makes the sign of the cross twice)*

OSVALDO: That's right. *(He starts to exit)*

SONIA: Wait. One last toast.

OSVALDO: To the bride?

SONIA: No, to us. *(She goes to the fountain to pour them champagne, and puts the potion into Osvaldo's drink)*

MIMI: Osvaldo?

OSVALDO: How dare you call me that!

MIMI: Okay, Daddy, is that better? This family is the only life I know. It exists for me.

OSVALDO: This is between your mother and me.

MIMI: No, listen, Daddy, the family is continuing. I'm going to make sure of that.

OSVALDO: How? Mimi, how?

MIMI: Never mind, Osvaldo.

Sound of car horn.

OSVALDO: She's honking the horn, hurry, Sonia!

Sonia hands Osvaldo the drink.

SONIA: Money, love and the time to enjoy it, for both of us!

OSVALDO: Thanks. *(He gulps down the drink and exits)*

MIMI: Osvaldo, you jerk. Bastard!

SONIA: Don't worry, Mimi, he's going to have diarrhea till sometime in March.

MIMI: Finally.

SONIA: Put the blame on me. I don't speak the right way. I don't know how to ask the right questions.

MIMI: That's not true, Mama.

SONIA: When I first got here . . . I got lost. I tried to ask an old man for directions. I could not find the right words to ask him the directions. He said to me, "What's wrong with you, lady, somebody give you a lobotomy?" I repeated that word over and over to myself, "lobotomy, lobo-tomy, lo-bo-to-meee!" I looked it up. It said an insertion into the brain, for relief, of tension. I remembered people who had been lobotomized, that their minds could not express anything, they could feel nothing. They looked numb, always resting, then I realized that the old man was right.

MIMI: No. Mama.

SONIA: So I decided never to communicate or deal with this country again. Mimi, I don't know how to go back to my country. He made me realize that to him, I looked like a freak. Then I thought, but I'm still me to Osvaldo, he's trapped too. He must feel the same way too. Put the blame on me.

Miriam and Oscar enter.

MIMI: Aunt Miriam, tell me, how did you find revenge?

MIRIAM: Against what?

MIMI: Your father.

MIRIAM: Oh, when my mother and father got to America, I made them live with me. I support them. Now they are old and they are dependent on me for everything.

MIMI: It's not worth it, Aunt Miriam.

MIRIAM: Yes it is.

MIMI: Grandma, I'm in the car.

MIRIAM: It's revenge.

OSCAR *(Shows Miriam the coke bottle)*: My revenge!

MIRIAM: Everyone in this family's got a drug.

MANUELA (*Enters*): Mimi is taking me home?
SONIA: Yes, Mama, she's waiting in the car—
MANUELA: You didn't do it right.
SONIA: I'm sorry, Mama . . . I did it the way I was taught.

Manuela kisses Oscar goodbye and then exits.

Why can't life be like it was? Like my coming-out party. When my father introduced me to our society in my white dress.
MIRIAM: Sonia, they threw the parties to give us away . . . perfect merchandising; Latin women dressed like American movies, doing Viennese waltzes. "Oh, beautiful stream, so clear and bright, a radiant dream we sing to you, by shores that . . . "
SONIA: I wonder what it would have been like if we would have stayed?
MIRIAM: They would have ridiculed us.
SONIA: We would have had a country.
MIRIAM: We didn't have a choice.

Oscar exits to the ballroom.

SONIA: Miriam, Pedro took his life because of that.
MIRIAM: No. Pedro did it because of days like today—afternoons like this one: when you are around the people you belong with and you feel like you're choking and don't know why. (*She takes out valium*) I'll give you a piece of magic.
SONIA: How many?
MIRIAM: One . . . no, two. A valium—that's the only certain thing. It reassures you. It lets you look at the truth. That's why psychiatrists prescribe them.
SONIA: You guarantee me Varadero? I'll be floating in Varadero Beach?
MIRIAM: If you take three you get to Varadero, Cuba.

Miriam and Sonia take the valium. From the offstage ballroom we hear Oscar speaking over the microphone.

OSCAR (*Sniff . . . sniff*): . . . One, two, three, testing, one, three, three, two, testing. Lenin or some Commie like that said that "you cannot make an omelet without breaking a few eggs." Funny guy. Testing. All right, now from somewhere in the armpit of the world, a little tune my mother taught me. (*He sings "Isla"*)

BROKEN EGGS

In an island
Far away from here
I left the life I knew
Island of mine
Country of mine
Mine and only mine
Terraces and houses
Country do you remember
Do you remember
Remember me?

MIRIAM (*Takes cushions from chair and puts them on the floor*): I want to float down Key Biscayne back to Varadero. Varadero, please, please come.

Miriam lies on the cushions. Sonia looks at her.

SONIA: Why is he making so much noise?!

MIRIAM: Shhh. I'm already there . . . miles and miles into the beach and the water is up to my knees . . . I float. The little fish nibble at my feet. I kick them. I'm in. I'm inside the place where I'm supposed to be.

OSCAR (*Singing offstage*):
You were once my island
I left you all alone
I live without your houses
Beautiful houses
Houses remembered.

SONIA: Sonia is not coming back. Cojimar, Sonia will never be back.

OSCAR (*Singing offstage*):
Eran mías
You were only mine
Never forget me
Don't forget me
Mi amor.

MIMI (*Enters*): Mama, what's she doing?

SONIA: Relaxing.

MIMI: Want to dance, Mama?

SONIA: Us?

MIMI: Yes.

SONIA: Yes.

OSCAR *(Singing offstage)*:
  En una isla
  Lejos de aquí
  Dejé
  La vida mía
  Madre mía
  Isla mía
MIMI: They're going to kick us out.
SONIA: That's all right, Mimi. I've been kicked out of better places.
OSCAR *(Singing offstage)*: Te dejé.

  *Sonia and Mimi begin to dance. Lights fade as we hear the end of
  the song.*

END OF PLAY